Land
OF THE
Giants

Land of the Giants

New York's Polo Grounds

Stew Thornley

Temple University Press Philadelphia

Temple University Press, Philadelphia 19122

Published 2000
Printed in the United States of America

♾ The paper used in this publication meets the requirements of the American National Standard for Information Sciences—Permanence of Paper for Printed Library Materials, ANSI Z39.48–1984.

Text design by Jim Gerhard

Library of Congress Cataloging-in-Publication Data

Thornley, Stew.
Land of the Giants : New York's Polo Grounds / Stew Thornley.
p. cm.
Includes bibliographical refrences (p.) and index.
ISBN 13: 978-1-56639-796-4 (cloth :alk. paper)
1. Polo Grounds (New York, N.Y.)—History. 2. Baseball—New York (State)—New York—History. 3. New York Giants (Baseball team)—History. I. Title.

GV416.N485 P648 2000
796.357′06′87471—dc21 00–041192

041508P

To Brenda

Contents

Acknowledgments

ANYONE DOING RESEARCH ON BASEBALL STADIUMS IS INDEBTED TO PHIL Lowry for his groundbreaking work in stadium research that resulted in the invaluable book *Green Cathedrals* (first published by the Society for American Baseball Research in 1986 and then by Addison-Wesley in 1992). In addition to gleaning information from *Green Cathedrals*, I had the opportunity to meet with Phil and benefit firsthand from his knowledge on stadiums in general and on the Polo Grounds in particular.

I owe special thanks to Society for American Baseball Research (SABR) members Dr. Seth C. Hawkins and John Pastier, stadium authorities who knew the Polo Grounds well, and who shared their memories and expertise. I am also grateful to Bob Bluthardt, Peter C. Bjarkman, and Lawrence S. Ritter for their advice and support, and to Ron Replogle, Bob Tholkes, and John McCormack for their proofreading and critiques.

Other SABR members who assisted in this project include Larry Zuckerman, David Nemec, Fred Ivor-Campbell, Ted Hathaway, Bob Harris, Michael Frank, Fred Stein, Kevin Cluff, Brenda Himrich, Fred Buckland, Jules Tygiel, George R. Rekela, Dennis Goldstein, Rob Edelman, David W. Vincent, Joe O'Connell, Clifford Blau, Richard Zitrin, Everett Parker, Andy McCue, Cy Morong, Jay Gauthreaux, Chuck Carey, Bob Tiemann, Steve Gietschier, Jay Roberts, Dan Levitt, John Gregory, Jim Wyman, Paul Rittenhouse, Bill Deane, Howard Luloff, Lyle Spatz, Kerry Keene, F. X. Flinn, John Thorn, David Lund, Mark Johnson, Stuart Leeds, Cary Smith, and Nancy Jo Leachman.

Jerry Schwab and Ed Logan took the time to tell me their tales of growing up with the Polo Grounds, which served as Ed's second home and Jerry's first.

Others who made contributions are Stan Isaacs and Larry Zwier; Corey Seeman, Bill Burdick, and Darci Harrington of the National Baseball Library and Archive; Don Majeski of the *International Boxing Digest;* Thomas Bourke of the New York Public Library; Tom Loudon and Gene Burns, historians of the Troy and Watervliet, New York, area; and Eileen M. Kennedy of the Museum of the City of New York.

Finally, I appreciate the constructive comments, advice, and help I have received from Ken Samelson of Masters Press, Dick Wentworth of the University of Illinois Press, Dan Ross of the University of Nebraska Press, Richard Peterson of Southern Illinois University Press, and, most of all, Michael Ames of Temple University Press.

Land
OF THE
Giants

CHAPTER ONE

Oddest of the Odd

IN ANY SPORT BUT BASEBALL, IDENTIFYING A SPECIFIC STADIUM BY THE diagram of its playing area would be difficult, perhaps impossible. Standardization is a staple in stadiums and arenas for sports like football, hockey, and basketball. But baseball, from the beginning, has felt less confined in determining its outer reaches. In the days before enclosed stadiums, a river or copse of trees could intrude upon a playing area. When fences were erected, it was for the purpose of charging admission to the game, and no standards existed for their height, their distance from home plate, or the shape they imposed upon the outfield.

Through most of baseball's history, the contours of its playing fields have been distinctive. Often it has been a matter of necessity. Ballparks wedged into the confines of existing city blocks emerged with strange shapes. Quirks in street schemes produced otherwise inexplicable crannies. Where a building remained because team owners were unable to acquire and demolish it, the outfield simply took a detour around it. The result is that baseball fans can tell where they are, whether it's Fenway Park in Boston or Wrigley Field in Chicago, by the idiosyncracies of the stadium. Sometimes just a glance at a stadium diagram is sufficient.

But even in a sport known for its curiously configured stadiums, one in particular stands out: the Polo Grounds, an odd name for an odd stadium, was home to several baseball teams, most notably the New York Giants until the team moved to San Francisco following the 1957 season. Its horseshoe-

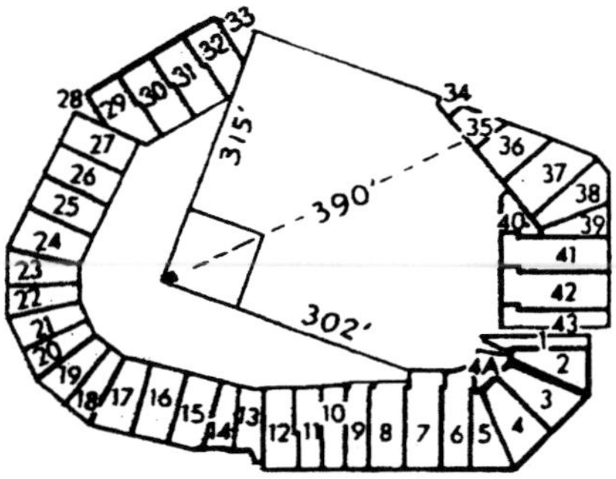

Fenway Park, Boston

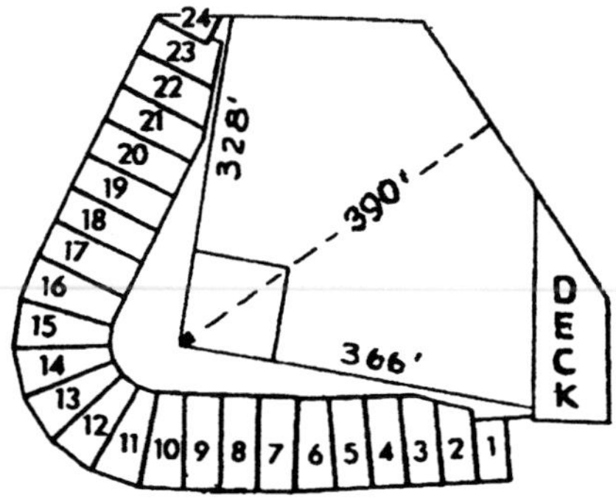

Crosley Field, Cincinnati

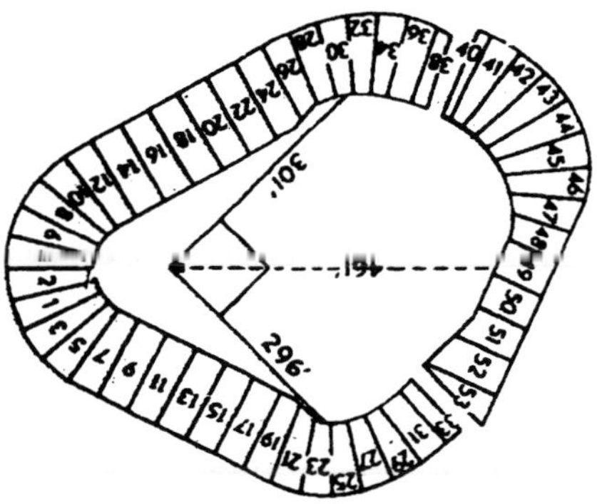

Yankee Stadium, New York

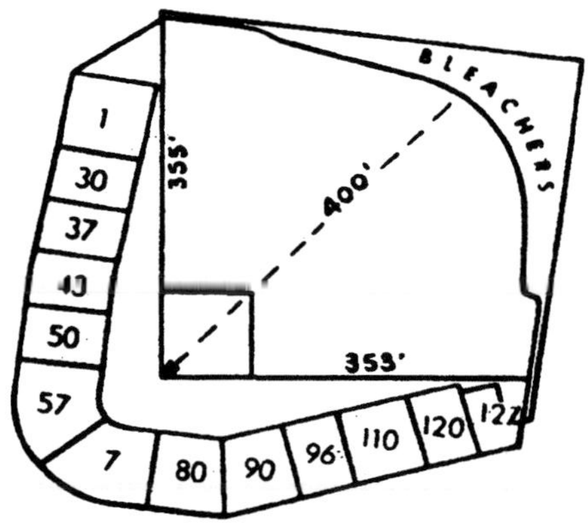

Wrigley Field, Chicago

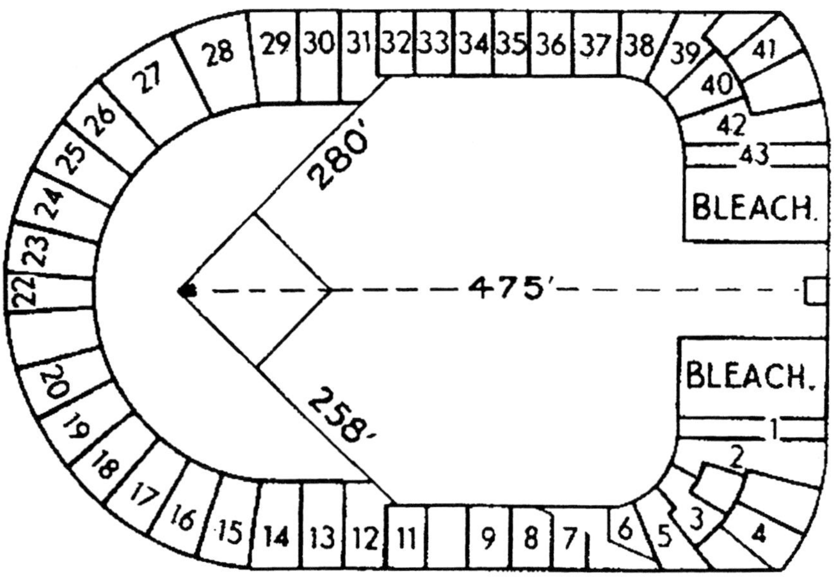

Polo Grounds, New York

shaped grandstand and elongated playing area provided for ridiculously short distances down the foul lines and equally ridiculous long distances to the power alleys and center field.

So short were its foul-line distances that inches were sometimes included in the measurements—279 feet, 8 inches, to left; 257 feet, 8 inches, to right. As for the distance to center, it was so long that the figure almost could have been rounded to the nearest hundred.

But there's much more to the Polo Grounds than its peculiar profile. Just as the New York American League team was identified with its home, Yankee Stadium, and the Dodgers in Brooklyn were known for Ebbets Field, the Giants were connected with the Polo Grounds. In some ways, it was easy to overlook the home of the Giants when compared to the grandeur of Yankee Stadium and the charm of Ebbets Field.

But in most other ways, the Polo Grounds was impossible to ignore—a massive edifice, tucked in between the Harlem River and an lofty outcropping of mica schist known as Coogan's Bluff. The vicinity of this escarpment in Upper Harlem (a portion of northern Manhattan) was originally part of a farm granted by the British Crown to John Gardiner in the early 1700s. It received its name after one of Gardiner's descendants, Harriet Gardiner Lynch, married James J. Coogan, a politician who would become Manhattan borough president in 1899.

When the New York Giants moved into Coogan's Hollow (the flat area below the bluff) in 1889, the area was considered the outskirts of town. Only in the past 30 years had the city even begun laying out streets on the eastern portion of Manhattan north of 155th Street, which was the southern boundary of the region. And it had also been barely 15 years since the area the Giants' stadium occupied was anything other than river-bottom wetlands that were more often than not covered with water. Landfill has been changing the size and shape of Manhattan ever since the Dutch arrived in the early seventeenth century,and the portion of land on which the Polo Grounds was built had evolved from the fill that had been dumped into the river.

But while its streets and, for that matter, its very turf, were relatively new, this part of town was served by public transit, providing a way for fans to get to the games. Elevated railroads first reached the area in the 1880s, followed by subways in the early twentieth century.

Fans had a choice in their approach to the Polo Grounds with regard to both direction and elevation. They could arrive outside the center-field area, exiting the subway station at 155th Street. Or they could approach the stadium from atop the bluff, having to descend a walkway, actually going downhill, to get to seats in the upper deck.

Beyond its structure and setting, the Polo Grounds is distinguished by the fact that some of baseball's most historic moments occurred here. They include one of the most memorable events ever, Bobby Thomson's home run to win the 1951 pennant for the Giants, as well as one of its greatest controversies, Merkle's Boner in 1908.

The Polo Grounds evoked emotions in the fans; some loved the place, others hated it.

Robert Creamer, the baseball historian and biographer of the game's stars, provided fodder for those in the latter category. "The Polo Grounds is a terrible place to watch a ball game," he wrote in 1963, citing the distance of outfield seats from home plate and the posts that ruined the view even from those seats closer in. According to Cramer, "Watching a game there is like watching it through a picket fence, and the people who sit there sway back and forth continuously during a game, first one way to get a glimpse of the pitcher winding up as the batter disappears behind a post—and then the other way, abruptly dismissing the pitcher, to watch the batter swing."

But Fred Stein, who grew up watching the Giants in the Polo Grounds and authored a book about the team, *Under Coogan's Bluff*, had a different opinion. "Despite the great distance from the bleachers to the plate and the fact that many seats were obstructed by pillars," he said, "the Polo Grounds was a great park in which to see a ball game."

Dr. Seth C. Hawkins is another man who spent much of his youth at the Polo Grounds. He's also an authority on what it's like to watch games in other places (having earned the nickname "Dr. Fan" because he has most likely attended major league games at more stadiums than any other fan) and continues to rate the Polo Grounds highly. One of the reasons for Hawkins's opinion is that the Giants had a policy of allowing fans with general admission tickets to sit in the last few rows of the lower grandstand behind home plate, rather than sending them to the far reaches of the outfield. "A broke kid could get there two hours before game time, when the gates opened," recalled Hawkins, "and if he could run pretty fast, he could get a seat behind home plate." Hawkins would enter at the outfield gate off Eighth Avenue and, once through the turnstiles, join the race with other young fans for the good seats. "It was a popular kids' pastime," Hawkins said of the dash from the area in right center field through the concourse to the sections behind home plate. "They recognized this was a deal they were not going to get at Ebbets Field and certainly not at Yankee Stadium."

Many recall the ballpark in a magical sense. Former major league pitcher John Curtis remembered: "The first big league game I ever saw was at the Polo Grounds. My father took me. I remember it so well—the green grass and green stands. It was like seeing Oz."

Garth Garreau became batboy for the Giants in the 1940s, an opportunity that grew out of his tryout with an American Legion team that used the Giants' stadium when the major leaguers were on the road. When Garreau asked where the tryouts would be held, his dad replied, "The Polo Grounds." As Garreau remembered, "I don't think he could have said any other three words that would have sounded so exciting."

And for some, the Polo Grounds was home. In the 1940s, groundskeeper Matty Schwab carved out a small apartment under the left-field grandstand for himself, his wife, and his young son, Jerry. As Jerry got older, he came to enjoy having the biggest backyard in New York City. He sometimes camped out in the outfield with friends, which included sons of Giant players and others who worked in the Polo Grounds. "Baseball was just there," said Jerry Schwab of living at the Polo Grounds. "For me it was like a God-given right. It was just part of my life. I didn't really think anything about it because it was all I remember. It was a great experience, and I didn't realize how fortunate I was at the time."

Like the fans, players had strong feelings—on both sides—regarding the Polo Grounds. Dead pull hitters, who could take advantage of the short distances down the foul lines, loved the place. Those with power to the alleys, though, thought of it as a hitters' graveyard.

Actually, the park was almost neutral in terms of being a hitters' or a pitchers' park. The narrowness of the stadium favored the defense, allowing outfielders to play close together and cut off drives to the gaps or corral flies that otherwise would have dropped between them for base hits. In addition, a great deal of foul territory was in play at the Polo Grounds, which made outs of some pop flies that would have safely reached the seats in other ballparks, thus giving the batter another chance.

But even though its record was about average with regard to total offense, the Polo Grounds was definitely a home run haven. Of all post-1914 stadiums, it remained the most likely place to see home runs until Coors Field in Denver opened in 1995. The short distances down the lines took in more short flies than the distant reaches of the power alleys kept out long drives. This advantage was enhanced by the upper decks, which overhung the lower in both right and left field. In right field, the upper deck facade was originally flush with the fence to the lower deck. But eventually a photographers' perch was added, causing it to extend forward by several feet. In right field this might not have been enough to create home runs out of pop flies that otherwise would not have made the seats in the lower deck, but in left field the overhang of the upper deck definitely could produce that result.

The frustrations the Polo Grounds could evoke in a pitcher, as well as in an outfielder waiting in vain for an easy fly to come down and settle in his glove, may never have been exemplified better than in a 1948 game, held right before the All Star break, between the New York Giants and their archrivals, the Brooklyn Dodgers.

The Giants took a 1–0 lead in the second inning on a Willard Marshall fly that dropped into the photographers' stand in right. Marshall was capable of reaching more distant places with his homers, but the peculiarities of the Polo Grounds were essential for Jack Conway, a light-hitting infielder who came to the plate in the ninth inning with the score tied 2–2. The first pitch from Brooklyn right-hander Willie Ramsdell nearly hit Conway in the leg. Many in the crowd of nearly 48,000 groaned at the near miss, realizing that gaining first in this manner may have been the most that could be expected of Conway.

But on the next pitch, Conway swung and lifted a fly to left. The Dodgers' rookie left fielder, George "Shotgun" Shuba, drifted back on the warning track and waited to take it in. But a gust of wind from the south pushed the ball a little farther out, causing it to hit the facing of the upper deck as it descended, giving Conway the only home run of his major league career and the Giants a 3–2 win. In his game account in the *New York Times*, Louis Effrat called Conway's home run "one of the most anemic homers ever hit in a park noted for 'cheap' circuit swats."

The subject of the effect of the Polo Grounds on hitters can consume baseball scholars. So can other features of the Polo Grounds, including the enduring nature of the ballpark's name. As the chapters that follow will reveal, the story of the Polo Grounds is actually the story of four stadiums. The final three were located beneath Coogan's Bluff, but the first stadium to use the name Polo Grounds, and the only one on which polo was actually played, was on the corner of 110th Street and Fifth Avenue, just north of Central Park.

The different Polo Grounds had their particular looks and characteristics, but all were places where fans came to see baseball. Mascots, electronic scoreboards with gaudy graphics, raucous music, and other distractions had not yet emerged in the days of the Polo Grounds. As Fred Stein said, "The menu at the Polo Grounds was strictly baseball, and that was the way we liked it."

CHAPTER TWO

The Original Polo Grounds

THE NATIONAL LEAGUE WITHOUT A BASEBALL TEAM IN NEW YORK. THAT unthinkable catastrophe took place following the 1957 season, when the New York Giants and Brooklyn Dodgers simultaneously abandoned the city for California.

But this had happened before. In 1876, the initial year of the National League, the New York Mutuals were expelled for refusing to complete their schedule. The Mutuals were losing money and opted to stop the financial bleeding by passing up their final road trip to the West, a trip that was meaningless to a team stuck in sixth place. But it wasn't meaningless to William Hulbert, the league's organizer. He expelled the Mutuals, along with the Philadelphia team, which had pulled a similar stunt, leaving the league with its integrity but without teams in the nation's two largest cities.

In a way, though, the National League hadn't really occupied New York, for the Mutuals had played their games at the Union Grounds in the still-independent city of Brooklyn. The Union Grounds had existed since 1862 and was the first field enclosed with outfield fences specifically for baseball use. In 1877 the Union Grounds had another National League tenant, a team that had moved from Hartford, Connecticut, and in fact retained the name Hartford Dark Blues. New York fans were understandably reluctant to support a team still identified with a city in a neighboring state, and the Hartford team disbanded after the 1877 season.

New York at that time was still 20 years away from the consolidation that created the five boroughs. The city was then essentially coterminous with the island of Manhattan, although it had recently annexed some portions of the area across the Harlem River in what would become the Bronx. In 1898 New York swallowed up Brooklyn, along with nearly 40 other townships and communities, to form New York City as it is known today.

It wasn't until 1880 that professional baseball was played in Manhattan. The site was a polo field in the midst of what was then a fashionable neighborhood dominated by aristocratic apartment houses and brownstones, just north of the northeast corner of Central Park.

Although polo had been played in some parts of the world for thousands of years, it didn't become popular in England until the mid-nineteenth century. It jumped the Atlantic when James Gordon Bennett, Jr., visited England and became captivated by the sport. Bennett, the son of the founder of the *New York Herald*, was by this time the owner and editor of the newspaper. One of his legacies is his decision to send reporter Henry Morton Stanley to Africa to find the missionary David Livingstone. But the younger Bennett achieved a greater reputation as a sportsman than as a newspaperman. According to *The Encyclopedia of New York City*, Bennett sponsored sporting events on land and sea as well as in the air in the form of regattas and races involving automobiles and airplanes. But the sport most linked with his name is polo.

While in England, Bennett had been a spectator at the Hurlingham Club in London, where English polo rules were codified in 1875. Returning to the United States the following year, he brought polo equipment and began teaching the game to his friends. That winter, he staged the first polo match, indoors at Dickel's Riding Academy in New York. Eventually Bennett moved the sport outdoors, to the large field he owned—bounded by 110th and 112th streets and Fifth and Sixth avenues—a four-square-block area he dubbed the "Polo Grounds."

Meanwhile, in 1880, two men captivated by a different sport were forming a partnership. One was John B. Day, a wealthy young merchant and Tammany politician who preferred to think of himself as a baseball player. The other, Jim Mutrie, was a man without Day's financial means but with a greater understanding of baseball.

"Smiling Jeems" Mutrie, a native of Chelsea, Massachusetts, had long been associated with baseball in New England as a player, manager, and team organizer. In 1880, following the collapse of an amateur team he had organized in Brockton, Massachusetts, Mutrie came to New York.

At the time, the area's main team was a Brooklyn club known as the Unions, which had been formed for the purpose of playing a series of games against a pair of visiting teams, the Nationals of Washington and the Hop Bitters of Rochester. The three teams played one another in several Brooklyn venues—the aforementioned Union Grounds; the Capitoline Grounds, which had been the home of the 1872 Atlantics of the National Association, the forerunner to the National League; and even a field at Coney Island—over an 18-day period in August. But when the Nationals and Hop Bitters left town, the Unions were left without an opponent.

A new team, called the New Yorks, was formed in 1880, with Jim Mutrie as its first baseman. But Mutrie had higher aspirations: he wanted to manage a team. He also felt that a new playing field would be needed. Even though Brooklyn was then the third-largest city in the country, it was separated by an estuary (the East River) from the country's largest city, New York. Mutrie fretted over the hordes of potential fans in New York who wouldn't make the effort to come to Brooklyn, since the only link between the two cities was a ferry. Cathedral arches were taking shape on the masonry towers of a bridge that was under construction, but completion of this span was still several years away. (Mutrie might have favored the idea of one legislator, who, during the debate over whether Manhattan should be consolidated with Brooklyn and other communities, proposed filling the East River with gravel to unite Brooklyn and Manhattan.)

Rather than worry about how to get the fans from Manhattan Island to Brooklyn, Mutrie decided to do it the other way around: he concluded that the ideal spot for baseball in New York was on the grounds being used for polo at 110th Street. He approached the polo club and secured a lease on the grounds for baseball—on the condition that he could get a financial backer.

Mutrie then began the task of attempting to persuade some of the city's upper crust to invest a small portion of their fortunes in a baseball team. His efforts paid off when he met Day.

With Day's money, Mutrie began to stock a roster with players from Brooklyn as well as the Rochester Hop Bitters, which had recently disbanded. Soon Mutrie had a squad of professionals, which he and Day called the Metropolitan.

The Metropolitans (normally referred to in the plural form even though Day and Mutrie intended the name to be singular) were an independent team, not affiliated with any league. They devised a schedule that would pit them against National League teams, once the league season was over. In the meantime, the Metropolitans played a collection of top amateur teams, including those from local colleges, and other independent professional teams.

In preparation for the team's arrival, work was underway to lay new drains and erect a grandstand on the Polo Grounds, but the facility wasn't ready as soon as Mutrie and Day had hoped. Instead, the Metropolitans continued playing at the Union Grounds in Brooklyn, with the team's first game occurring on Thursday, September 15, 1880.

The first game on the Polo Grounds was scheduled for Wednesday, September 29, against the Nationals of Washington, the team that a month earlier had been making the rounds in Brooklyn. More than 2,000 fans turned out for the first professional baseball game in New York City. They almost went home disappointed, as the Nationals didn't show up on time. Finally, more than a half-hour after the game's scheduled starting time of 3:30, the Nationals arrived through the Sixth Avenue gate. The late start made it impossible to complete nine innings, but the Metropolitans, behind the pitching of Hugh "One Arm" Daily, defeated the Nationals, 8–3, in six innings. (Some sources place the final score at 4–2, not bothering to count the runs scored by both teams in the last inning played, which was cut short by darkness.)

Over the next month, the Metropolitans played National League teams, primarily at the Polo Grounds, although scheduling conflicts (including some polo matches) forced the team to return to the Union Grounds in Brooklyn as well as a field in Hoboken, New Jersey. However, Day was able to work out arrangements with the Manhattan Polo Association, which agreed to leave the field on 110th Street free for the Metropolitans starting with the following season.

In 1881 and 1882, the Metropolitans continued playing a mix of amateur and professional opponents, including National League teams whenever possible. The team remained independent during this time despite an invitation to join a newly formed major league, the American Association, in 1882.

A series of events following the 1882 season resulted in New York getting teams in the American Association *and* in the National League. It began when two teams, in Troy, New York, and Worcester, Massachusetts, were forced to resign their memberships in the National League. The teams represented the two smallest cities in the league, and drawing fans was never easy for either of them. Troy (which at the time played on an island in the Hudson River) had only 12 fans at one of its final games in 1881. The next year, even though the team was playing in a different stadium, on the mainland, it again struggled with attendance. It was no different in Worcester. The team's final game in the major leagues, on September 28, 1882, was played before a crowd described by the *Boston Globe* as "about two dozen."

With the resignation of Troy and Worcester, the National League had a pair of openings for the 1883 season. One of the vacant spots was filled by Philadelphia. It was expected Day would fill the other by entering the Metropolitans in the National League, but instead accepted the American Association's offer, a year after it had first been made, and also announced he would produce a another team, from scratch, for the National League. To do this he turned to the defunct Troy team and signed its top players. The very best he kept for his National League team; the next echelon were relegated to the Metropolitans.

First baseman Roger Connor, catcher Buck Ewing, and pitcher Mickey Welch ended up with the National League team, which initially was known simply as the "New-Yorks." Some sources indicate that the team's original nickname was Gothams, but this appellation was not used in newspaper accounts. The top Troy player to end up with the Metropolitans was pitcher Tim Keefe. Thus even though the Troy team was unable to survive, it did produce some great players for a pair of other franchises down the Hudson River. (Connor, Ewing, Welch, and Keefe are now members of the Baseball Hall of Fame.) Jim Mutrie remained with the Metropolitans as manager.

The year 1883 was a momentous one for New York. The Metropolitan Opera was beginning, and the great bridge spanning the East River between Lower Manhattan and Brooklyn Heights was about to open. It was this link, the Brooklyn Bridge, that facilitated commerce and traffic between two great cities. Had it opened three years earlier, John B. Day might not have sought alternate quarters for his team.

But he had, and as a result the first of several baseball stadiums named the Polo Grounds was about to serve as the home to two major league teams, the first to play their home games within the confines of New York City.

CHAPTER THREE

Major League Baseball in New York

FANS TRANSPORTED THROUGH TIME BACK TO 1883 WOULD STILL RECOGnize the game of baseball but would notice many changes in the rules. Pitchers then stood 50 feet from home plate, 10 1/2 feet closer than at present, but were restricted in how they could go about their business. Overhanded delivery was not yet permitted, and hurlers did what they could with a snap of the wrist as they released the pitch from below the waist. Batters could call for the location of their pitch—above or below the waist—but it took eight pitches out of the strike zone before they could take a base on balls.

Fielders for the most part did their work barehanded, although gloves were becoming more common. Not surprisingly, errors were abundant.

Rosters were smaller, in part because of a rule prohibiting substitutions unless a player was disabled by injury or illness. The style of pitching also produced less strain on a hurler's arm, which, combined with the much smaller number of games played in a season, meant a team did not need a large rotation; for some teams, two pitchers worked an entire season. (This was the case for the Metropolitans in 1883 and 1884. Tim Keefe and Jack Lynch handled almost the entire load for the team, pitching in all but 1 of the Metropolitans' 209 games over that two-year span. Lynch, by the way, had pitched in the first baseball game on the Polo Grounds on September 29, 1880, when he was the losing pitcher for the Washington Nationals in the game against the Metropolitans.)

Although baseball in 1883 had many differences from the modern game, the diamond had a familiar look. Bases then, as now, were 90 feet apart, as they had been ever since that distance was set by the Knickerbocker Base Ball Club of New York in the 1840s.

By the 1880s, however, baseball had experienced a total departure from the standards of sportsmanship set in the 1840s, when the game was predominantly a sport played by gentlemen's clubs. For starters, the behavior—of both the teams on the field and the fans in the grandstands—was worse in the American Association than in the National League. The American Association was founded primarily to evade the National League's stringent rules, including the prohibition of the sale of alcohol on the grounds. In addition to selling beer, American Association teams charged only 25 cents for admission—half the amount it took to get into a National League game.

Cities with major league teams at the time were primarily in the north and east and mostly in larger cities. The American Association had a team in Columbus, Ohio, with a population barely more than 50,000, but the National League, with the departure of Troy and Worcester, no longer occupied any city with fewer than 100,000 residents.

In 1883, Providence, Rhode Island, was the smallest city in the National League, New York the largest. In between were Detroit, Buffalo, Cleveland, Boston, Chicago, and Philadelphia. The American Association had teams in Louisville, Pittsburgh, Cincinnati, Baltimore, St. Louis, and Philadelphia, in addition to Columbus and New York.

In New York, the Polo Grounds was by this time no longer being used for polo. Baseball was the only sport on the site, and the grounds contained a lavish and expansive double-decked wooden grandstand in the southeast corner of the rectangular lot, near the intersection of 110th Street and Fifth Avenue. Including the bleachers that extended beyond the grandstand, down the left- and right-field lines, the Polo Grounds had as many seats as any stadium in baseball at that time.

In those days, a ballpark's capacity was not confined to the seats. Large crowds often spilled onto the field, sometimes in fair territory, where they would shrink the playing area and reduce the distance of the outer boundaries from home plate. The Polo Grounds, especially in left field, had a lot of distance to reduce. In this direction, the grounds extended nearly all the way west to Sixth Avenue, which left outfielders with plenty of room to track down long drives. Even when the crowds weren't excessive, fans arriving in horse-drawn conveyances were allowed to park in deep left field and watch the game from the comfort of their carriages. However, they were kept so far out that they rarely affected balls hit in that direction.

During this period, the primary function of fences was to keep out non-paying fans, not to delineate a home run. In fact, the foul lines at the Polo Grounds did not even reach the outfield barriers. At the end of the lines, serving as foul poles, were posts rising out of the ground, with colorful flags at the top. Most home runs of the day were inside the park, especially at the Polo Grounds.

The New York teams prepared for the 1883 season with a series of exhibition games in April. Because of a peace accord between the two leagues, reached only two months before, preseason games between National League and American Association teams were allowed. As a result, the New-Yorks and Metropolitans played eight games on the Polo Grounds. More than 5,000 fans turned out for their first meeting.

But that crowd was puny compared to the turnout two-and-a-half weeks later, when the National League season opened on the Polo Grounds with a game between New York and Boston on Tuesday afternoon, May 1. "The residents of Harlem were awakened from their usual state of quiet and repose yesterday afternoon by seeing immense crowds of people coming up town on their way to the Polo Grounds," reported the *New-York Tribune* in its next-day's edition. From all directions came the fans, taxing the capacity of the Second, Third, and Sixth Avenue elevated lines.

The gates of the Polo Grounds opened at 2:00, and a stream of humanity poured in. By the time the game began two hours later, the crowd was in excess of 15,000. Many fans could scarcely see any of the players, much less the game itself. One fan who did get a decent vantage place was General Ulysses Grant, who sat in the rear of the grandstand.

Buck Ewing and Jack Burdock, the respective captains for New York and Boston, tossed for choice of innings. Boston won the toss and elected to take the field, sending the New-Yorks to bat first. Moments later, Ewing stepped to the plate to begin the rich history of major league baseball at the Polo Grounds. Boston hurler Jim Whitney, unconcerned about such history, struck Ewing out. Whitney then got two strikes on Roger Connor, New York's powerful first baseman, before Connor connected on a long drive to right field, good for three bases and the beginning of a three-run rally.

New York built a 6–0 lead and held on, behind the pitching of Mickey Welch, for a 7–5 win. Grafulla's Seventh Regiment Band, which had entertained the fans before the game, returned to the field and played "See the Conquering Hero Comes" as the fans continued with a prolonged ovation for the victors.

Connor's first-inning drive was the nearest thing to a home run in the opening game, and he came close to hitting the first home run in the Polo

Grounds the next afternoon. Boston again had Whitney in the pitching box, but the New York hurling duties fell to John Montgomery Ward, who had played center field the day before.

The game was tied, 2–2, with one out in the last of the ninth, when Connor sent a long fly beyond the outfielders toward Sixth Avenue. A faster runner might have ended up with a home run, but the slow-footed Connor was ruled out at the plate, a decision not popular with the fans, who had already spent the better part of the afternoon disagreeing with umpire S. M. Decker's calls. Ward then stepped in and sent a drive to almost the same location as Connor's hit. Ward, having greater speed, was able to complete the entire journey around the bases safely, arriving home with the game-winning run and the first major league home run in the history of the Polo Grounds.

The New-Yorks were off to a great start on the Polo Grounds. (Contemporary newspapers more often referred to games *on* the Polo Grounds rather than *at* the Polo Grounds.) However, the Metropolitans, managed by Jim Mutrie, didn't fare nearly as well in their home opener.

The first problem concerned the team's playing area. John B. Day's plan to solve the issue of having two major league teams but only one field was to carve out separate diamonds at opposite ends of the lot. He intended on having the New-Yorks play on the diamond in the southeast corner and the Metropolitans on a diamond toward the southwest corner. As the *New York Clipper* of February 17, 1883, had reported:

> The chief feature will be the erection of a new and handsome grand-stand in the southwest corner of the field, near where the club-house now stands. It will be built in the most substantial manner and will be of a semi-circular shape, the centre section seating 1,000 persons and the two wings each seating 750 persons. A number of private-boxes and a stand for reporters and scorers will be placed on the roof of the grand-stand.

Portions of the grandstand from the existing diamond of the Polo Grounds had been moved over to the west side in March. However, the southwest diamond and grandstand still weren't ready for the Metropolitans' scheduled home opener on Saturday, May 12. The Metropolitans instead played on the southeast diamond, before a crowd only one-fifth the size of that at the opener for the New-Yorks. The Metropolitans, and the team's star pitcher, Tim Keefe, were battered by the Athletic Club of Philadelphia and lost their home opener by a score of 11–4. Over the next two-and-a-half weeks, the Metropolitans continued to play their home games on the southeast diamond while work continued on the southwest diamond.

The Polo Grounds were being used for all types of baseball events at the time. On the rare days that neither the National League nor the American Association team was using the grounds, college and other amateur teams played there. (This continued through later versions of the Polo Grounds. Colleges, high schools, and a number of other amateur teams were allowed use of all the stadiums that bore the Polo Grounds name. In September 1947, the *New York Times* even listed an upcoming charity baseball game between the "Arm Amputees vs. Leg Amputees.")

Near the end of May 1883, a special exhibition took place, with the Metropolitans facing a picked nine (a group of individual players assembled for a particular game rather than an already intact team). A crowd of 4,000 turned out, mainly to see the Metropolitans' pitcher, bareknuckle heavyweight champion John L. Sullivan. "Sullivan has always been identified with base-ball," reported the *New-York Times*, "and at one time was a promising player. He has been practicing curves and up and down shoots lately, and it is said they will prove as effective as his round hitting." For his performance with the Metropolitans, Sullivan received 50 percent of the gate receipts, although many wondered if he had actually earned his keep. Sullivan did not attempt to pitch hard, claiming he was afraid of spraining his arm. The *New-York Tribune* reported: "The contest was a farce from beginning to end and the crowd was thoroughly disgusted. . . . Sullivan's delivery was neither swift, accurate, curved, nor effective." Nevertheless, he continued to pitch for various teams, and draw large crowds, in exhibitions throughout the Northeast the rest of the season.

Usually baseball games on the Polo Grounds took place one at a time. However, during a two-week stretch beginning May 30, Decoration Day (the original name of Memorial Day), both the New-Yorks and Metropolitans were at home. Fortunately, the west diamond was finally ready for occupancy by this time, although the Metropolitans quickly learned that it was a far inferior playing area (with some of the tract reportedly leveled with the use of raw garbage as landfill). However, the Metropolitans had little choice, because five games—involving five major league teams and two college squads—were scheduled for the Polo Grounds on Decoration Day, and two diamonds would be necessary to accommodate all of them.

The Metropolitans started the long day of baseball with a 9:30 A.M. game against Cincinnati, a contest that marked the opening of the west diamond at the Polo Grounds. A half-hour later, just a bit to the east, the New-Yorks began a game against Detroit.

When the National League game was over, Yale and Princeton took the field on the east end for a game to decide the college championship. Upon its conclusion, the New York and Detroit teams returned for the second game of their doubleheader. Meanwhile, the Metropolitans—who had eked out a 1–0 win over Cincinnati in the morning game—were beating Columbus, 12–5, to complete a doubleheader sweep over two teams. The crowds were sparse for the early games, but fans came and went over the course of the day, and, in all, upward of 10,000 spectators turned out to see at least some of the baseball at the Polo Grounds on Decoration Day.

In an attempt to quell some of the confusion of simultaneous games, Day had a flimsy, canvas-covered fence erected to separate the playing areas. This portable fence remained up through June 14, during which time the New-Yorks and Metropolitans continued to play on opposite ends of the same grounds at the same time.

The Metropolitans then left on a long road trip and didn't return to the Polo Grounds until July 23. By this time, the New-Yorks were ready to begin a road trip. Both teams were at home in August, but usually at different times. At the end of August, though, the schedule once again called for a brief stretch when both New York teams were to play at home at the same time. The portable canvas-covered fence was reinstalled as games were played simultaneously on the opposite diamonds.

Under rules of the day at the Polo Grounds, balls rolling under the fence remained in play, causing the bizarre scene of an outfielder emerging into the opposing field in pursuit of a ball. Although outfielders proved agile and adept at getting under the fence to reach the fugitive balls, occasionally a hit that rolled under the fence ended up as a home run.

In addition, the canvas fence restricted the field of play to the point of producing some cheap over-the-fence home runs. A few batters even adjusted their batting style to take advantage of the easy reaches. Of the August 30 game between the New-Yorks and Boston, the *New-York Tribune* said, " 'Sky-scrapers were more numerous than 'daisy-cutters.'. . . . There was little scientific place batting. The adjustable fence separating the League from the American Association field again retarded the movements of the players, and some of the runs would never had been made had the grounds been larger. The Polo Grounds are sufficiently large for one game of baseball, but not nearly large enough for two games to be played at once." In this game, Boston's John Morrill came to the plate with two runners on in the first inning and sent a drive—one that might have been catchable if New York left fielder Pete Gillespie had had unlimited room to roam—over the barrier in left field for a three-run homer. The next day, John Montomery Ward of the New-Yorks countered with a similar drive for a home run. A few days later, the canvas-covered fence was removed for good.

(I am still unclear on how often the west diamond on the Polo Grounds was used by the Metropolitans in 1883—if it was normally used by the Metropolitans or if it was used only when there was a scheduling conflict on the east diamond because the New-Yorks were at home at the same time. Some researchers maintain that the Metropolitans normally used the east diamond and moved to the west diamond only on the 12 dates when there was a conflict on the east diamond. However, I am not convinced this was the case. It seems that the original intention of John B. Day [who owned the Metropolitans as well as the New-Yorks] was to have the Metropolitans play regularly on the west diamond in 1883. This is based on reports from the *New York Clipper* during the first three months of 1883 in addition to an item that appeared in *The World* [New York] on Saturday, May 12, 1883, the date of the Metropolitans' first regular-season home game. *The World* reported that the Metropolitans were playing their home opener on the east diamond because the west diamond was not yet ready, implying that they would be using the west diamond regularly when it became available. However, it is possible that the Metropolitans—after their first round of games on the west diamond, from May 30 to June 14—were so discouraged by the condition of the field that Day decided to abandon the west diamond, use it only when there was a conflict [as there was again later in the season, between August 30 and September 4], and have the team play most of its games on the east diamond. It is clear that the first games were played on the west diamond on Decoration Day, May 30; it is also clear that, regardless of the situation, the portable fence was used to separate the two playing areas only when both the Metropolitans and New-Yorks were home at the same time.)

Neither the New-Yorks nor the Metropolitans challenged for their league title in 1883, although the Metropolitans did finish in fourth place, two spots higher than their counterparts in the National League, and did even better in 1884.

However, the Metropolitans started the 1884 regular season in a different stadium. Complaints from visiting teams about the arrangements on the Polo Grounds in 1883, along with the desire of Association officials to have the team loosen its ties with the New York National League franchise, prompted the American Association to order the Metropolitans to find a new stadium. Over the winter, John B. Day settled on a site between 107th and 109th streets along the East River and had the lot prepared for baseball. It would be accessible by the Second and Third Avenue elevated lines as well as by water, as arrangements were made with the Harlem Steamboat Company to stop at landings near the ballpark on days games were being played. The

New York Clipper of February 2, 1884, reported, "It is expected that the new grounds of the 'Mets' will be the handsomest in the country."

Rather than being a step up, however, the move was a distinct step down. Metropolitan Park, as the new stadium was named, was built on a site formerly occupied by the city dump. It proved to be such a foul location that it made even the west diamond of the Polo Grounds look like a palace. Pitcher Jack Lynch said of the ballpark, "A player may come out of the dressing room as frisky as a two-year-old colt, go down for a grounder, and come up with six months of malaria."

There was more to Metropolitan Park's noxiousness than merely being a former dump. "It was so close to numerous factories across the East River that foul smoke made it dangerous for fans," said Philip J. Lowry in *Green Cathedrals*. (Relegating the Metropolitans to second-class surroundings was in line with the way Day normally operated the team, according to David Nemec, author of a history of the American Association, *The Beer and Whisky League*. Nemec has written that Day treated the Metropolitans as "kind of an afterthought" and that he "ran the Mets on a shoestring to the point that its players, bereft of equipment, stole bats from opposing teams, especially Cincinnati, a well-endowed team.")

A good crowd turned out for the first game at Metropolitan Park, on Tuesday, May 13, 1884, to see Tim Keefe and the Metropolitans defeat the Allegheny Club of Pittsburgh. "The diamond was well sodded and presented a neat appearance," reported the *New-York Times*. "It is beautifully laid out and afforded the spectators a good view of the game." The review in *The World* wasn't as kind, pointing out that the neighborhood of Metropolitan Park "at present is by no means a choice one" and adding that "the ground is filled in and the filling is of such a nature as to be decidedly unpleasant to the olfactory organs."

The malodorous conditions at the games proved too much for fans to endure and the crowds became sparse. After only five weeks, Day gave up on Metropolitan Park as the regular home for his team. When the Metropolitans returned from a month-long road trip in mid-July, they moved back onto the Polo Grounds.

The southwest diamond at the Polo Grounds was no longer being used, and the Metropolitans began sharing the southeast diamond with the New-Yorks. However, there were a few scheduling conflicts on the Polo Grounds during the remainder of the 1884 season; when this happened, the Mets ended up going back to Metropolitan Park. One game there, on August 7, was postponed because of the poor condition of the grounds.

Day searched for another backup facility and tried to secure Washington Park, home of the Brooklyn team that had joined the American Association that season. With the Brooklyn Bridge now connecting the two great cities, Day was comfortable with hosting a handful games across the East River. An August 10 game between the Metropolitans and Baltimore was scheduled for Washington Park, but rain postponed the contest. No Metropolitan home games ever were played at Washington Park, and the team continued to go to Metropolitan Park when the Polo Grounds wasn't available.

Through all the turmoil, the Metropolitans kept winning and were atop the standings in the American Association. The leader in the National League was the Providence Grays, a team that had played the Metropolitans in a series of preseason exhibition games on the Polo Grounds in April. Even though Providence had won all three games, Metropolitan manager Jim Mutrie was eager for another chance. He challenged Providence to an exhibition game in August, an invitation that was turned down, as was a later offer for a postseason meeting between the teams. Not until Mutrie popped off to the newspapers, claiming that Providence was afraid to play them, were the Grays shamed into accepting the challenge. Mutrie might have been better off keeping his mouth shut, as the Grays swept the Metropolitans in three games, all of which were played on the Polo Grounds in late October. (Even though the champions of the American Association and National League had met in a postseason series in 1882, this 1884 matchup between the Metropolitans and the Grays was considered the first "World's Series" that was sanctioned by both leagues. This arrangement continued through most of the remaining seven years of the American Association's existence, although there was never a fixed system for the format of the series; the number of games—which at one point was as high as 15—was determined each year by the champion teams, and the locale was not restricted to their home fields or cities.)

Even though the Metropolitans had been swept in the World Series, Day was pleased with their play and felt he had a good team on his hands—too good, in fact, to be playing in a league that charged only a quarter for admission. He decided to consolidate his best players on his National League team, for which he could charge the citizens of New York 50 cents for the privilege of watching.

The first move Day made was to transfer his manager, Jim Mutrie, from the Metropolitans to the New-Yorks. Shifting his top players, however, would require a bit more finagling. Rules established by the leagues required a 10-day waiting period before released players could be signed by other teams. Day was determined to get Dude Esterbrook and Tim Keefe, the Metropolitans' top hitter and pitcher, respectively, to the New-Yorks. He knew other teams would be eager to talk to these players once they were released and wanted to keep those teams away during the waiting period. His solution was to sequester Esterbrook and Keefe by sending them on a cruise, with Mutrie as a chaperone. As soon as they departed, Day released Esterbrook and Keefe from the Metropolitans. The pair became eligible to sign contracts with the New-Yorks on Monday, April 6, at a time when they were still in Bermuda with Mutrie. When the trio returned to the United States, Keefe and Esterbrook were members of the New York National League team. The American Association was outraged and even suspended Mutrie for his part in the shenanigans. It was an empty suspension, however, since Mutrie by this time was no longer a part of the Association.

Rumors abounded that the Metropolitans were on the verge of collapse, although Day strongly denied it. "There is no truth in the report that the Metropolitans are going to disband," he stated on April 10, 1885. "The Mets will play all their scheduled championship games, and I do not hesitate in saying that they will make a strong fight for first honors. I have paid out considerable cash in advance money, and it isn't likely that I would disband the club at this stage of the season."

The Metropolitans opened their home season on the Polo Grounds before 3,500 fans on Friday, April 25, and raised a large pennant made of white bunting, with a border and letters of blue, bearing the inscription, "Metropolitan, 1885, Champions." (Even though the championship was won in 1884, the pennant carried the date 1885.)

The Mets and New-Yorks shared the Polo Grounds again in 1885. Normally, one team was playing elsewhere when the other had a game at home, but, as had happened the previous two seasons, there were a few occasions when both were scheduled for the Polo Grounds. The conflicts had been resolved in 1883 by having the Metropolitans use the west diamond on the Polo Grounds and in 1884 by having the team go back to Metropolitan Park. In 1885, though, the Metropolitans and New-Yorks shared the Polo Grounds on the same day by playing doubleheaders. The Metropolitans would play their opponent at 1:45 or 2:00, with the New-Yorks following with their game. The pace of games was much more rapid in the 1800s, and it was normally possible for both games to be completed with existing daylight, even late in the season and even though daylight saving time was more than three decades away. Fans enjoyed the opportunity to see both teams for the price of one admission, even though they had to pay the usual National League charge of 50 cents rather than the cut-rate American Association fee of 25 cents.

The fortunes of the two New York teams reversed themselves in 1885. Robbed of their stars, the Metropolitans languished. As the recipient of those stars, the New-Yorks were able to compete for the National League pennant for the first time. After the New-Yorks beat Boston on the Polo Grounds on August 28 (following a game between the Metropolitans and the Athletic Club of Philadelphia on the Polo Grounds), the New-Yorks had pulled within a half-game of the Chicago White Stockings. It was, however, as close as they would come, as Chicago held on to finish the season two games ahead of New York, which had a won-lost record of 85–27. Meanwhile, the Mets finished in seventh place in the American Association with a record of 44–64.

The New York National League team didn't pull off a pennant in 1885, but it did wind up with a nickname, one that both the fans and newspapers were picking up on. It had actually begun to be used a few days before the season started, during an exhibition game, when Jim Mutrie exhorted his team by hollering, "Come on, you giants." He also referred to his players as "his big fellows" and "his giants." Before long the team itself was being known as the Giants, and one of the most famous names in sports was born.

Mutrie was immensely popular with New Yorkers and had another phrase—"We are the people!"—that was a hit with the fans at the Polo Grounds. Fred Engel, a batboy for the New York team at the time, recalled that Mutrie "would arrive at the park dressed formally—high hat, tails and all—and parade around the park shouting, 'Who are the people?' Without waiting for a reply, he would scream, 'The Giant fans are the people.' The fans cherished him." The feeling extended to the rest of the Giants, many of whom lived at the Broadway Central Hotel on Broadway. "They would travel to the old Polo Grounds in an open, horse-drawn carriage to the resounding cheers of the fans who lined the streets," Engel remembered.

As for the fans, even then the Giants were attracting a distinctive bunch to their games. Into the twentieth century, the Giants were the New York team most of the theatrical crowd followed, a tradition begun back in the 1880s. Following a Giants' win over Detroit on July 22, 1885, John B. Day attributed the victory to the presence of his guests—the company of *The Black Hussar*, a comic operetta that was playing at Wallacks Theater on Broadway and 13th Street. The cast members in attendance included DeWolf Hopper, who became best known for his frequent recitations of Ernest L. Thayer's poem "Casey at the Bat," and Digby Bell, who had been a member of the Knickerbocker Base Ball Club in the 1860s.

A later Polo Grounds regular wasn't a member of the city's theatrica crowd, but Frank B. Wood—a fixture at New York sporting events who constantly blurted "Well! Well!"—made enough of an impression on writer Zane Grey (himself a baseball player of some ability) that Grey based a character on him in the tale "Old Well-Well," which appeared in Grey's anthology *The Redheaded Outfield and Other Baseball Stories.* "He was Old Well-Well, famous from Boston to Baltimore as the greatest baseball fan in the East. His singular yell had pealed into the ears of five hundred thousand worshipers of the national game and would never be forgotten," wrote Grey. However, the ear-piercing shouts of the real "Well! Well!" did not sit easily with nearby fans, who complained and eventually had Wood barred from the Polo Grounds for many years.

The Giants were the team to see in New York, and there was little room for another, especially a decimated group like the Metropolitans. At the end of the 1885 season, the Metropolitans were sold to a man named Erastus Wiman, who operated the Staten Island ferry and owned an amusement park on Staten Island. Over the next two years, before the team was completely dissolved, the Metropolitans played their games at a facility within the amusement park called the St. George Cricket Grounds. Not only was a round-trip ferry ride included with the price of admission to a Metropolitans' game, but during the final half of the 1886 season, fans in the top row could turn away from the game and watch the erection of the Statue of Liberty.

With the Metropolitans gone, the New York Giants became the sole baseball tenant of the Polo Grounds starting in 1886. They continued as a popular attraction and became the first team to draw a crowd in excess of 20,000. It occurred in the afternoon game of a morning-afternoon doubleheader between the Giants and Detroit on the Polo Grounds on Monday, May 31, 1886. The Giants won the morning game, 6–5, in 10 innings. "When the fact [of the morning win] became known about town," reported the *New-York Times,* "the Polo Grounds acted like a loadstone."

So many fans were clustered when the gates opened for the afternoon game that the three regular entrances were overwhelmed, and the carriage entrance and employee door also had to be opened. The grandstand seats were quickly sold out, and spectators took to the field and found a place to stand in the sun. By 3:30, an hour before the scheduled start of the afternoon game, every available space outside of the playing lines was occupied.

"When the time finally arrived for the players to don their uniforms and begin the contest, they found the diamond occupied by the surging mass," continued the story in the *Times:*

> By this time just 20,632 persons had passed through the gates. Besides this numbers of small boys had scaled the fence, and the hundreds of knotholes in the fence that

> surrounds the large grounds were plugged up by youthful eyes whose owners' pockets could not stand the strain that would necessarily have been imposed upon them had they passed through the gates. When the gong sounded for the players to begin the contest, they could not find standing room, let alone take their positions in the field. The police worked like Trojans in their efforts to put the crowds back. But it was impossible. They stood in the diamond and on the bases and would not move back an inch. Finally the base line was cleared and the game began.

That, however, was not the end of the commotion. The crowd surged forward as New York batted in the last of the first inning, forcing the players to retire to their dressing rooms. Police on foot and horseback were able to clear the infield, but little playing area remained beyond that. The teams finally agreed to continue with the provision that fair balls hit into the masses would count only as singles. The Detroit batters proved to be more adept at working the overflow for ground-rule singles and ended up winning the game.

Although crowds of this magnitude were rare, this type of scene—fans encroaching on the playing area and even stationed in fair territory—occurred with some regularity in the 1800s and continued (although it became less common as stadiums with larger seating capacities were built) all the way into the 1940s.

The New York-Detroit doubleheader was played on May 31—rather than May 30, the customary date for Decoration Day—because the holiday fell on a Sunday in 1886, and Sunday baseball still wasn't allowed in New York City (nor would it be for another 33 years). The Sunday ban did not apply just to the professionals. The previous year, newspapers had reported on youths being arrested and fined for playing baseball in both Harlem and Brooklyn. The issue of Sunday baseball was being debated elsewhere as well. At this same time in Ohio, a test case involving Fleet Walker—who, in 1884, as a member of the Toledo team of the American Association, became the first black to play major league baseball—was wrapping up. Although Walker was acquitted on the charge of playing baseball on Sunday, the legality of Sunday baseball was left unsettled.

While Fleet Walker, along with his brother, Welday, had a brief career in the major leagues, dark-skinned players were definitely the exception in organized baseball in the 1880s. This was true at the Polo Grounds as well, although blacks were welcomed in certain roles—mascot, for example. Buck Ewing, the Giants' captain and catcher, found black mascots to be a good luck charm. Ewing's penchant, as well as the way it was reported in the newspapers, provides a revealing look at racial attitudes in the late nineteenth century. The *New-York Times* of Monday, August 3, 1885, included this note:

> Ewing's mascotte [*sic*], the colored boy, who is admitted to the Polo Grounds every day free of charge to satisfy the superstitious whims of the players, was rubbing [Mickey] Welch's arm with a strong liniment before the game on Saturday [which the Giants won]. "Boys," he said to the players, "I earned $4.50 last week. I received my cash this morning, and I've bet it on the game. My whole fortune is on it. If you lose, I don't eat to-morrow." After the game the colored boy received the players at the clubhouse with open arms. His eyes fairly danced in his head, and displaying two rows of ivories, he yelled joyfully, "Boys, I eat chicken to-morrow."

Ewing produced a different mascot a few years later and had the lad lug his catching equipment onto the field before an important game against Boston. Reported the *New-York Tribune:* "As the Giants neared the grand stand the applause changed to wild roars of laughter. Carrying Captain Ewing's body-protector and mask was probably the blackest mascot that ever was born. The young colored lad appeared to be the happiest darkey in the world. He was dressed in the regulation New-York uniform and was black enough to frighten away all the witches and 'hoodooes' in Harlem."

The Polo Grounds was a difficult place in which to hit home runs in the mid-1880s. (*Total Baseball* lists the home run factor for the east diamond as 71, with 100 being average; this means that home runs were reduced by nearly 30 percent on the original Polo Grounds because of the characteristics of the ballpark itself.) However, the Giants had a slugger capable of reaching not just the outfield fences but the property fences that provided the outside border to the stadium itself. Roger Connor became the first batter to hit a home run entirely out of the Polo Grounds on September 11, 1886. He accomplished the feat off Boston's "Old Hoss" Radbourn, sending a drive entirely over the right-field stands and into a field across 112th Street. "He met it squarely and it soared upward with the speed of a carrier pigeon," reported the *New-York Times*. "All eyes were turned on the tiny sphere as it flew over the head of [Charlie] Buffinton in right field, and when it finally disappeared over the fence a shout of joy went up from the 2,600 spectators." According to Bernard J. Crowley, "Connor was the premier power hitter of the 'Gaslight Era' " and, according to legend, the main man that Jim Mutrie had in mind when he began referring to his team as giants.

Roger Connor wasn't the only dangerous hitter in the New York lineup in those years. The entire team got into the act in a 29–1 win over Philadelphia on the Polo Grounds in June of 1887. Mike Tiernan had six hits and scored six runs in addition to moving from his normal spot in center field to take the mound and pitch the final four innings (holding Philadelphia hitless during his pitching stint). The action was apparently too exciting for one spectator, as the *New-York Times* noted that a horse dropped dead on the field during the game. "Manager Mutrie remarked that the animal probably came from the Quaker City," reported the *Times.*

The Giants were successful during this period because they had sturdy batsmen as well as pitchers who could stifle strong hitters from opposing teams. No one stifled them better than Tim Keefe in 1888. Over a seven-week period from late June to mid-August, the New York right-hander set a major league record by winning 19 consecutive games. Behind the pitching of Keefe and Mickey Welch, as well as the slugging of Connor and the performances of players like catcher Buck Ewing, shortstop John Montomery Ward, and outfielders Silent Mike Tiernan and Orator Jim O'Rourke, the Giants won their first National League pennant and advanced to the World Series against the St. Louis Browns of the American Association. New York beat the Browns, six games to four, in a series played in New York, St. Louis, Brooklyn, and Philadelphia. Four of the first five games of the series were played in New York and turned out to be the final games ever played on the original Polo Grounds.

For some time, there had been indications that the city might be planning on extending 111th Street, which at this point had been interrupted by the Polo Grounds between Fifth and Sixth avenues, through the site occupied by the Giants. John B. Day, a man familiar with the workings of New York City politics, had been able to hold off the move for a while (reportedly through yearly bribes of season tickets to the Board of Aldermen), but in early 1889 the city announced it would proceed with its plans. Day made a few efforts to further delay the demise of the Polo Grounds but finally gave up.

Ultimately, 111th Street ended up going right through the heart of the field, and the elaborate grandstand was torn down and replaced by a traffic circle—one eventually named for public administrator James J. Frawley. Meanwhile, the Giants were left to seek new quarters as the 1889 season approached.

LONGINES
ALWAYS BUY CHEST

A panoramic view of the Polo Grounds as Gil McDougald of the Yankees hits a grand-slam home run in the 1951 World Series. The top of Yankee Stadium is visible above the open bleachers to the right of the clubhouse in center field. All images not otherwise attributed are from the author's collection.

Mickey Welch at bat against Boston's "Old Hoss" Radbourn in 1886.

BASEBALL IN NEW YORK CITY.—A GENERAL VIEW OF THE POLO GROUND, WITH A MATCH GAME IN PROGRESS.

FROM A SKETCH BY STAFF ARTIST.—SEE PAGE 2[illegible]

This view of the Polo Grounds appeared in Frank Leslie's Illustrated Newspaper *in June of 1888.* Collection of Fred Buckland

The New York and Philadelphia teams line up in front of the grandstand of the Polo Grounds before the first game of the 1888 season, the final year for the original Polo Grounds.

This woodcut of the New Polo Grounds, in the southern portion of Coogan's Hollow, appeared in Frank Leslie's Illustrated Newspaper *shortly after the ballpark opened in July of 1889. Note the steep embankment in center field.* Collection of Fred Buckland

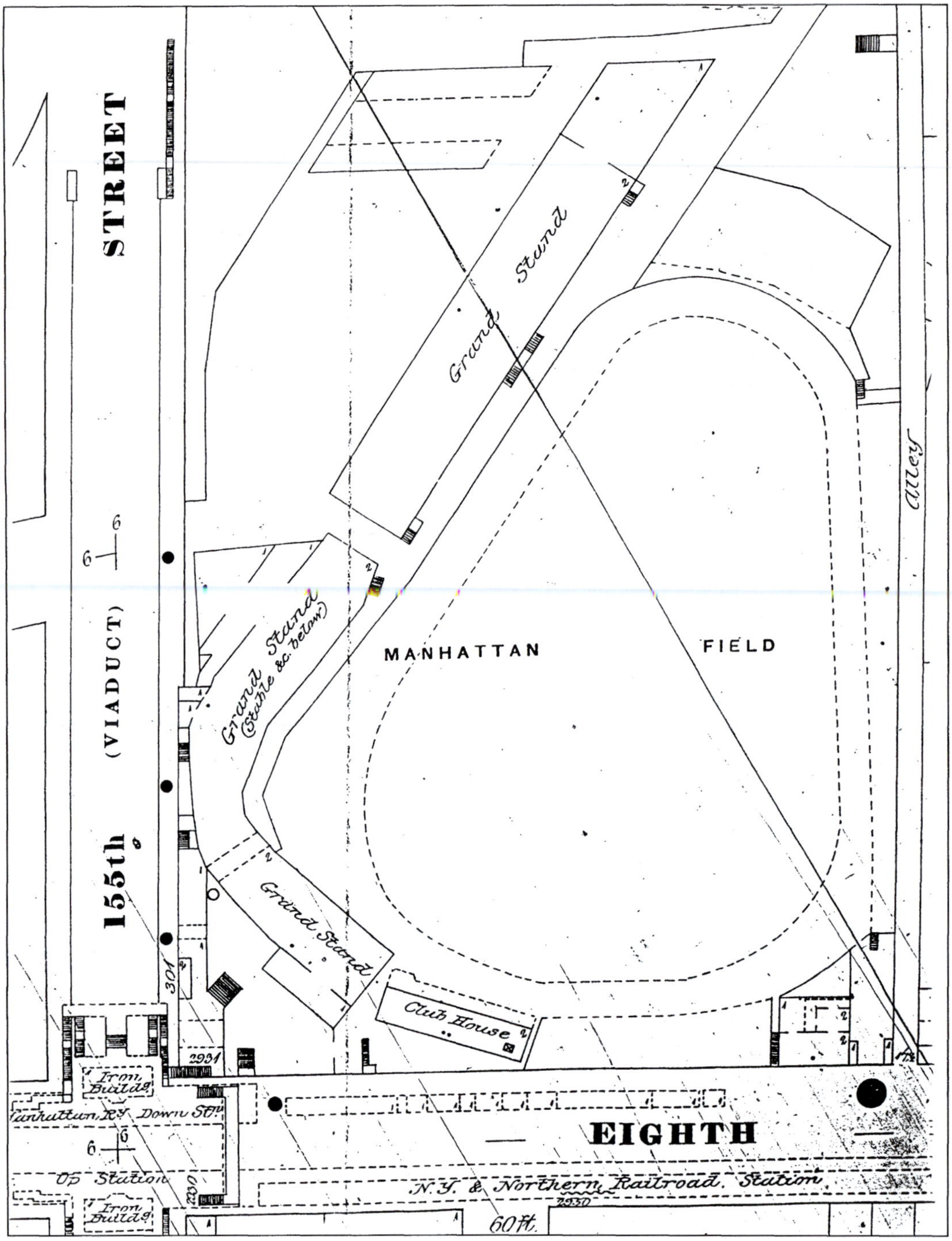

A map of Manhattan Field in 1894. The shape of the playing field had changed from the time it was used by the National League Giants in 1889 and 1890.

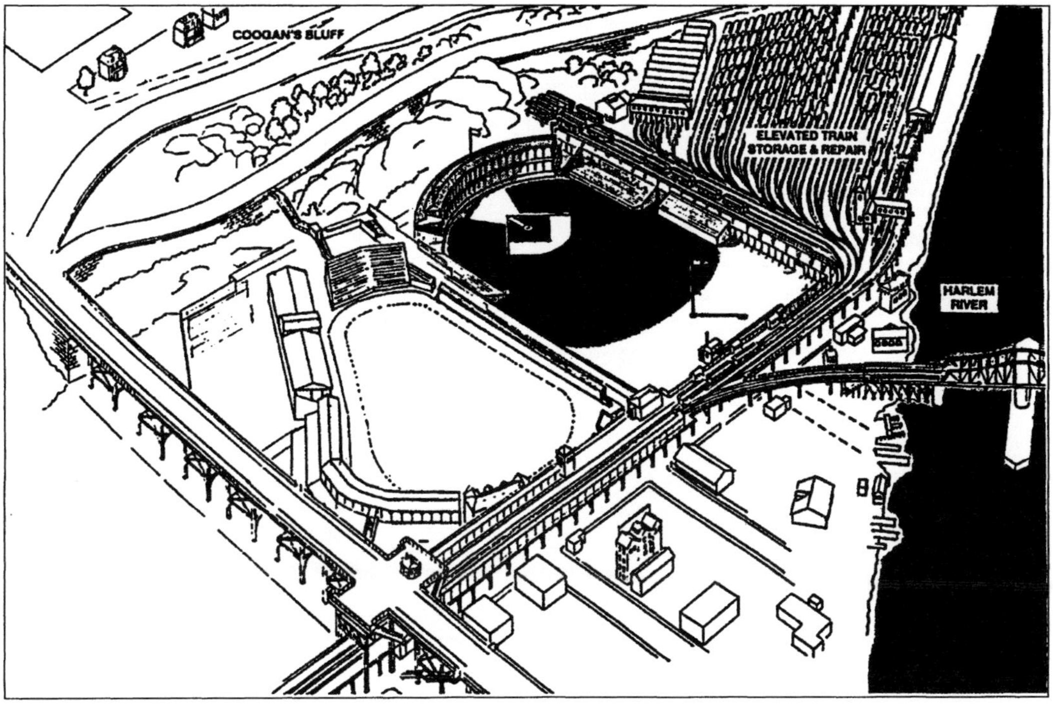

A new ballpark opened immediately to the north of the New Polo Grounds in 1890. Originally used by the New York team in the Player's League and known as Brotherhood Park, it was taken over by the National League Giants in 1891 and renamed the Polo Grounds. The stadium they had abandoned reverted to the name Manhattan Field. Its grandstand remained for several years, and the playing area was used for a variety of activities.

FOR
LADIES
AND
GENTS
GO TO
KELLY'S
FOR

This photograph focuses on Manhattan Field but also shows a portion of the Polo Grounds to the left. In the background is the Macombs Dam Bridge, which opened in 1896. Museum of the City of New York

WASHINGTON HEIGHTS

Coogan's Bluff is visible in the background as fans watch the 1905 World Series from center field.
Collection of Lawrence S. Ritter

John McGraw took over as manager of the Giants in 1902 and led the team to 10 pennants.
Collection of Lawrence S. Ritter

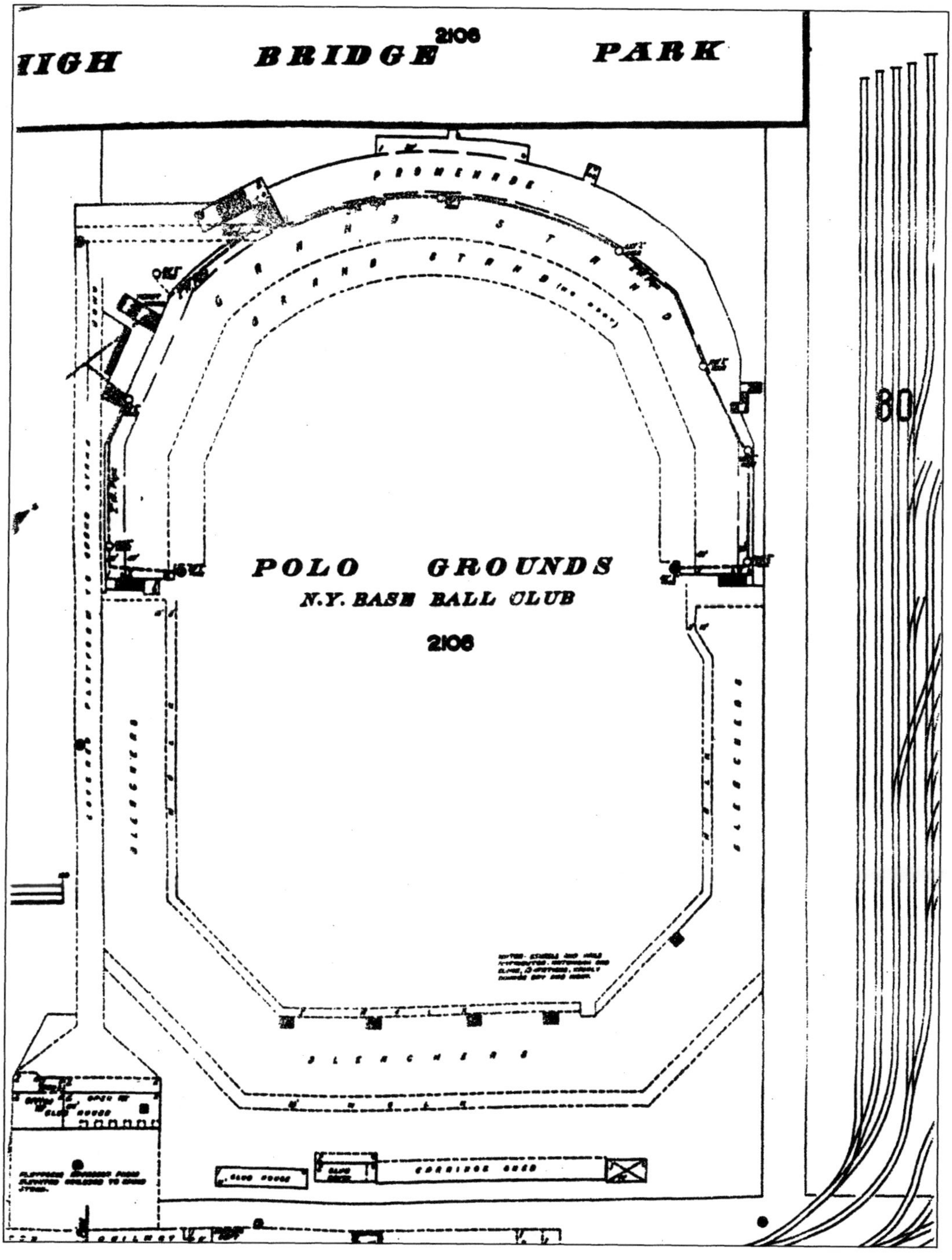

A 1908 map of Polo Grounds III, the first of the so-named stadiums to assume the peculiar bathtub shape.

CHAPTER FOUR

New Location, Same Name

HAVING STILL NOT SETTLED ON A PERMANENT LOCATION FOR HIS GIANTS by the time the 1889 season opened, John B. Day arranged for the use of a ballpark across the Hudson River in Jersey City. After only two games there, though, Day moved the team to another set of temporary quarters, the St. George Cricket Grounds on Staten Island, the same facility used by the Metropolitans in 1886 and 1887.

The Giants met some mighty challenges on Staten Island. The previous year the outfield area had been used for a theatrical production, leaving it bereft of grass. Scaffolding for the backdrop of the stage was still up, in some parts infringing upon the playing field. It also turned into a soggy spring in the East in 1889. Heavy rains contibuted to the great Johnstown flood in Pennsylvania. It was a bit drier in the vicinity of New York City but still wet enough that the outfield on the St. George Cricket Grounds became a virtual swamp, requiring parts of it to be covered with planks to provide traction for the fielders. Although the weather improved in the latter part of the spring, attendance didn't pick up for the Giants on Staten Island, and Day accelerated his efforts to find a permanent home for his team.

Finally, on Friday, June 21, Day settled on a location just off the Harlem River in the southern half of Coogan's Hollow in Manhattan, a lot that ran 400 feet west beneath the 155th Street viaduct and 460 feet north along Eighth Avenue. Even though he didn't need it at the time, Day was considering leasing more land from the Lynch estate, owners of the property. By the end of the season, he would lament the fact that he hadn't.

The parcel of land that he did lease, known as Manhattan Field, had been used for baseball and other activities during the 1880s, but at this point it was far from being in the condition necessary to host a major league baseball team. Work began immediately with the grading of the property and the erection of fences, while arrangements were made to move some portions of the grandstand and "bleaching boards" from the original Polo Grounds on 110th Street to the new location. Most of the grandstand would be completely new, however, and the architect hired to design the new stadium was the same one who had done the plans for the grandstands at the Philadelphia Base Ball Grounds and the magnificent South End Grounds in Boston, which both opened in the late 1880s.

Work was briefly delayed a few days after its commencement when a dispute arose over the ownership of the property. One morning Day and his contractor arrived at the site to find a gang of men digging postholes and fencing off several lots on the property, reportedly upon the orders of a Cleveland man named A. L. Johnson, who claimed to own the property. The dispute was quickly settled as James J. Coogan, executor of the Lynch estate, clearly established his ownership. The foreman of the interlopers said he would return with authority to continue his work. However, the man never appeared again, and the conversion of the lot to a major league baseball stadium continued.

Day was concerned about confusion that might be present with fans as the team prepared for its third home of the season. He knew that New Yorkers associated the name Polo Grounds with his baseball team, and so—to send an unambiguous message as to where the Giants would be headquartered—he christened the quarters the "New Polo Grounds." The sport of polo had never been—nor ever would be—played on this site, but nonetheless the name endured. (In keeping the familiar name, Day started a New York trend later followed when the name Madison Square Garden was retained for arenas built away from the vicinity of Madison Square.)

The entrance to the New Polo Grounds was approximately 40 feet from the stairway of the Eighth Avenue elevated station on 155th Street. Behind this, work was proceeding on a new Macombs Dam Bridge that, when completed in the mid-1890s, would provide greater accessibility for fans from across the Harlem River in what was to be the Bronx. The original bridge on this site, built as a dam in 1813 to operate a mill, was partially destroyed in 1838 by indignant citizens who objected to the fact that it blocked a navigable stream.

Just north of the Macombs Dam Bridge was the Putnam Bridge, which carried the Eighth Avenue elevated trains across the river. This bridge remained until the 1950s, when it was no longer needed because of the demise of the elevated system in Manhattan. A bit farther upstream was the High Bridge, completed in 1842 as a means of carrying the Croton Aqueduct across the Harlem River. The Macombs Dam Bridge, an extension of the 155th Street viaduct, remains today, as does the High Bridge, which, although no longer functional, has been placed on the register of national historic landmarks.

Access to the area was good enough for a huge throng to turn out for the first game at the New Polo Grounds, on Monday, July 8 (barely more than two weeks after work had begun to convert the field into a stadium). Over time, the facility became more elaborate, and it eventually featured a double-decked grandstand behind home plate and a large clubhouse behind first base. In addition, the area under the third base grandstand included horse stables.

For the first game, though, the grandstand and bleachers could accommodate only about 5,000 fans. As was the custom of the times, many fans took up spots in the playing area, and the total attendance—within the stadium—exceeded 10,000. DeWolf Hopper, by now developing a following for his recitations of "Casey at the Bat," was among the fans fortunate enough to secure a spot within the grounds. Upon entering, Hopper immediately indicated his approval of the new facility by letting loose with a blood-curdling war whoop.

Many of those denied access retired to a beer garden across the street, an establishment that offered at least a partial view of the game through its windows. A larger group occupied the high ground to the west of the stadium. This area—officially Coogan's Bluff—was dubbed "Dead-Head Hill" by the *New-York Times*, which observed that the onlookers from the hill "were bunched together as closely as chocks in a dude's trousers."

Edward "Cannonball" Crane was one of the heroes of the 7–5 New York win over Pittsburgh in the first game at the New Polo Grounds. The Giant pitcher started a four-run rally in the third inning with a single. On the mound, he overcame a bad leg (saying after the game that his "knee cracked like a rusty hinge" every time he delivered the ball) and outhurled Pittsburgh's venerable James "Pud" Galvin, a pitcher who already had won more than 300 games in his career and is today a member of the Hall of Fame.

Ensconced in their new home, the Giants were determined to repeat as National League champions. Their main rival was Boston, with a big series between the teams set for the Polo Grounds at the end of August. The grandstand was virtually complete by this time, and the largest crowd to date at the

New Polo Grounds turned out for the opener of the three-game series on Thursday, August 29.

The game was barely underway when it was brought to a momentary halt by a panic in the crowd, brought about by the settling of a portion of the balcony. Accompanied by the sound of cracking timber, the settling—caused by the shifting of a pair of cross-beams—created a rush for the stairways and the front part of the grandstand, with many among the throng ready to jump over the railing. Policemen and the players, bats in hand, waved the crowd back and got the spectators to return to their seats without anyone being trampled. Boston won the game, 6–4, to open up a three-game lead over the Giants.

Behind Tim Keefe, New York evened the series the next day, before a much smaller crowd. Building inspectors were reluctant to let fans back into the upper deck, afraid not so much of a collapse of the grandstand but rather of another panic should the beams shift again. By the following day, however, the inspectors were convinced that the stands would hold up, and more than 14,000 fans crammed into the Polo Grounds to watch Boston and New York battle to a 9–9 tie in a game stopped by darkness after eight innings.

Like the other stadiums that had and would bear the same name, the Polo Grounds at 155th Street and Eighth Avenue was oddly shaped. Narrow on the west end and bulging toward the east, the playing area resembled a pear. Home plate was in the southern part of the lot, with first base extending toward the Harlem River and third base toward Coogan's Bluff. The outfield featured a embankment running from center toward right field. Outfield embankments were not unusual in early baseball stadiums, but this one stood out because of its size and steep pitch. It created difficulty for the outfielders who had to patrol the area, particularly when rains made the embankment muddy and the footing treacherous.

Such was the case in that year's final regular-season game at the Polo Grounds, on September 14, 1889, when Chicago's Capt. Adrian Anson hit a long drive to center. The ball, rather than rolling back down, stuck in the top of the embankment, which was too slick for New York center fielder George Gore to climb. Unable to reach the ball, Gore watched helplessly as Anson circled the bases with a home run. However, the Giants still won the game and continued their winning ways as they went on the road the following week, finally moving into first place ahead of Boston. The two teams stayed close to one another the rest of the way, with the Giants finally pulling out the pennant on the final day of the regular season.

Once again, they advanced to the World Series against the Brooklyn Bridegrooms. (Brooklyn, which would join the National League the following season, had forsaken its nickname of Trolley Dodgers in deference to several players on the team who had gotten married late in the season and, for the good of the team, had practiced abstinence during the stretch drive.) Celibate or not, the Bridegrooms were no match for the Giants, who knocked off the champions of the American Association, six games to three.

In 1890, Brooklyn moved from the American Association to the National League, which meant that Brooklyn and the New York Giants would have the chance to play one another more frequently and develop one of the most heated rivalries in the history of sports. However, this rivalry was already being acknowledged when the teams met in the 1889 World Series. "The rivalry between New-York and Brooklyn as regards baseball is unparalleled in the history of the national game," reported the *New-York Times* on the eve of the series.

If the close proximity of the teams wasn't enough to cause strife between them, some of Brooklyn's tactics in the World Series created hard feelings among the Giants. All three of the Bridegrooms' wins in the series were in games that were stopped short of nine innings because of darkness. The Brooklyn players were prone to stalling while in the lead in these games, delaying play as much as possible until there wasn't enough light left to continue. The Brooklyn methods didn't sit well with the Giants. "The days of such tactics are gone by," said New York manager Jim Mutrie after Brooklyn won the third game of the series, 8–7, in eight innings at the Polo Grounds. "It comes with poor grace from the Brooklyn men to resort to them. Such methods are disgusting and do not tend to elevate the national pastime. . . . I would sooner lose a game than win as they did this afternoon." When Brooklyn stalled and won again the next afternoon, Giants' captain Buck Ewing had his say: "I am sick and tired of the methods resorted to by the Brooklyns. We have played like men, but the Brooklyns have disported themselves like schoolboys. Their work throughout has been of the sneaky order. They have made use of tactics that my men would not stoop to."

After losing three of the first four games, the Giants reeled off five straight victories—none of which was shortened by darkness—to win the series. Although owner John B. Day rejoiced in another world title, he was concerned about events taking place off the field.

A new league, the Brotherhood of Professional Base Ball Players, an organization with its roots among members of the New York Giants, was in the process of forming. The Brotherhood had been created in 1885 as a means of thwarting a salary cap plan the National League owners attempted to implement, with John Montgomery Ward of the Giants elected as Brotherhood president and New York pitcher Tim Keefe as its secretary. The Brotherhood and the National League were able to coexist over the next few seasons, but in 1889—in response to further abuses by the owners—Ward and his followers made plans to form a league of their own for the following season.

News of the rebel league broke in September of 1889, while the Giants and Boston were fighting for the pennant. On top of that, James J. Coogan revealed that "capitalists and men interested in the New York Club [slated for the new league] have approached him with offers to lease certain lands just north of the Polo Grounds for baseball purposes." No doubt John B. Day was sorry he had not leased the northern portion of Coogan's Hollow when he had had the chance; instead, it ended up in the hands of the owners of the New York team in the Players' League, which the new organization was called. The backers, Edward A. McAlpin and Edward B. Talcott, began work on a new baseball stadium, Brotherhood Park, next door to the Polo Grounds.

The Brotherhood's battle was with the National League owners *in toto;* however, Ward and many of the Giants retained warm feelings toward their owner, John B. Day. Ward even offered Day an executive job in the Players' League. Day remained loyal to his fellow owners, though. Without the support of the owner of the team in the nation's largest city, the National League itself may have collapsed. Day helped to save the league, although he would pay dearly for it personally.

Some of the Giants, most notably Mickey Welch and Mike Tiernan, were unable to desert Day. Most of the others, though, solidly supported the Brotherhood and joined the New York Giants of the Players' League.

The 1890 season in New York opened with games being played simultaneously in the adjacent stadiums, Brotherhood Park to the north and the Polo Grounds to the south. Fans demonstrated which version of the game they wanted to watch. With Roger Connor, Tim Keefe, Jim O'Rourke, and player-manager Buck Ewing on the New York Players' League team (Ward himself had become player-manager for the Brotherhood team in Brooklyn), larger crowds turned out in the northern ballpark. The *New-York Times* reported the attendance at Brotherhood Park as 12,013, well more than the crowd of 4,644 at the Polo Grounds for the National League game. Day stated that when the novelty of the new league wore off, the fans would come in larger numbers to see his team play. It wasn't to be. The disparity in attendance grew worse. One Saturday, with both teams playing at home simultaneously, the Brotherhood game drew 6,000 fans, while barely 200 were present at the Polo Grounds for the National League game. The National

League Giants, after having drawn more than 200,000 fans in 1889, dropped to a season attendance of barely more than 60,000 in 1890 and needed help from other National League owners merely to continue operations through the year.

Stripped of its top players, the National League Giants finished in sixth place. The team still had a few stars and provided a few exciting moments for the fans, few as they might have been, who did turn out. On Monday, May 12, 1890, the National League teams of Boston and New York staged a tremendous battle that was enjoyed by the 687 fans at the Polo Grounds in addition to some of the 1,707 fans who had come to watch the Boston and New York Players' League teams play in Brotherhood Park.

The game at the Polo Grounds featured a pair of young pitchers now in the Hall of Fame: 20-year-old Charles "Kid" Nichols for Boston and Amos Rusie, who was approaching his nineteenth birthday, for New York. "Both did magnificent work," reported *The World* the next day. "The two youngsters kept sawing away without let down, while the perspiration dropped from their foreheads as the game progressed. There probably is no equal to this game in baseball annals so far as the pitchers are concerned." The game remained scoreless through 12 innings as both the pitchers and fielders shined.

As the Giants came to bat in the top of the thirteenth inning (the home team having its choice of whether to bat or take the field first at that time), they had some additional spectators. Some in the crowd at the Players' League game had gotten wind of the duel unfolding next door. They moved to the top of the bleachers on the south side of Brotherhood Park, where they could peer over the fences and into the Polo Grounds.

After Nichols struck out Rusie to start the thirteenth, Mike Tiernan broke up the shutout with a tremendous drive to center field that cleared the fence of the Polo Grounds, landed in the narrow alley that separated the two ballparks, and bounded up against the outer fence of Brotherhood Park. As Tiernan circled the bases with what would be the only run of the game, he received lusty cheers from fans in both parks. "Never before in the history of the game have the same number of people shown so much enthusiasm on a ball field as there was shown at the New Polo Grounds yesterday when Tiernan knocked the ball over the centre-field fence, winning the game for the New-Yorks," wrote the *New-York Times*. "Even the people who were at the Brotherhood game, and who were watching the League game at the top of the fence, made a great demonstration. And why not? Tiernan had done what few people ever believed could be accomplished. The ball struck the fence of Brotherhood Park."

Coogan's Hollow was a busy spot for baseball in the summer of 1890, with teams from two leagues making their home there. In addition, a new Brooklyn team in the American Association (one that replaced the Brooklyn Bridegrooms, who had jumped to the National League and were in the process of winning a league pennant for the second straight year), the Brooklyn Gladiators, used the Polo Grounds for some of its home games in late July and early August.

Following the 1890 season, a treaty of sorts was established between the National League and the Players' League that brought about the elimination of the latter. The rebel organization left a number of legacies, however, including the financial ruin of John B. Day and a new ballpark for the Giants.

Having lost his fortune fighting to keep the Giants afloat and the National League together, Day was forced into an alliance with the men who had backed the Brotherhood efforts in New York. Although Day remained briefly as president of the team, his power was all but gone. Eventually his health went the way of his wealth, and Day died in virtual poverty in 1925, a pension granted to him by the National League a few years before being all that kept him and his wife from becoming charges of charity.

The new group of owners decided that Brotherhood Park, now without a tenant, was the superior facility in Coogan's Hollow and moved the New York National League team into it for the 1891 season. The Giants were making another move uptown, although this one was only a matter of feet rather than blocks. And, once again, with the Giants came the name of their stadium, as Brotherhood Park was renamed the Polo Grounds.

The New Polo Grounds (which thus became the *old* Polo Grounds) on 155th Street reverted to its previous name, Manhattan Field, and was leased to Andrew Freedman, another man with Tammany Hall connections who would eventually take over the Giants. At Manhattan Field, the grandstand that had been built for the Giants remained through the decade. Even after it became nothing more than a vacant lot, it remained the site of cricket matches and other sporting events in addition to serving as a parking lot for the Polo Grounds. Although Giants' management leased the parcel to other interests for a variety of uses, the team—with a fresh memory of the 1890 interlopers building a ballpark next door—retained control of the property to ensure such an event never happened again.

CHAPTER FIVE

Polo Grounds III

The third stadium named "the Polo Grounds" was changing even before it became the Polo Grounds. During the 1890 season—when it was still Brotherhood Park—the stadium was undergoing a massive makeover that increased its capacity and redefined its dimensions.

Two small bleacher sections were erected in center field, while other bleacher sections, those reaching out from the grandstand, were extended into fair territory. The result was a reduction of the distances down the foul lines—from 335 feet to 277 feet in left field and from 335 feet to 258 in right field. Center field remained approximately 500 feet from home plate, far enough away that the well-to-do could park their horse-drawn carriages beyond the ropes that delineated the playing area and watch the game from there.

With these modifications, and the takeover of the stadium by the National League Giants, Polo Grounds III became the first of the so-named stadiums to assume the distinctive horseshoe shape for which they would be known. Although over time this configuration would be viewed as odd, Phil Lowry in *Green Cathedrals* wrote that the Polo Grounds was in fact "more regular in its form than many parks of its era."

The grandstand was double-decked, with the roof supported by Y-shaped posts, and curved around home plate and approximately 20 feet past first base and third base. For a time in the early 1900s, the configuration of the diamond was such that a portion of the curving grandstand protruded across the foul line and into fair territory in right field. A white line was painted on the front fence of the curving grandstand and a pole was erected on its far edge. The line and the pole, which aligned with one another, served as markers to separate fair from foul territory. Beyond this protrusion was an alcove used for the bullpen, with the outfield bleachers (which contained still another foul pole) beyond. Balls hit into the fair territory portion of the bullpen were in play. Balls hit along the same path but not as far could land in the section of the grandstand extending into fair territory. The batter would not receive a home run for his efforts, however, since the rules dictated a minimum distance of 235 feet for an over-the-fence home run; instead the drive would result in a double. Still, the protruding grandstand was a strange feature that made it possible for a ball to be hit too far to be a double.

The first National League game in Polo Grounds III was played on Wednesday, April 22, 1891, and a huge crowd was on hand to see the Giants reunited. Before the game, Giants who had remained with the National League team lined up on one side of the field with those who had gone to the Players' League standing on the other. The two sides then came together to indicate that past differences had been settled and that they were one team again.

The Polo Grounds was in fine condition for the event. "The emerald infield is closely cropped and looks as level as a billiard table," was the report from the *New-York Daily Tribune*. A pair of pitchers destined for the Hall of Fame—Amos Rusie of New York and John Clarkson of Boston—were on the mound for the first National League game in the park. Clarkson and Boston came out on top, winning 4–3. But despite their opening day disappointment, the Giants put on a good show for their fans in 1891, rising to a third-place finish.

The American Association, which had operated as a major league since 1882, disbanded after the 1891 season. The National League absorbed four of the Association teams, swelling its ranks to 12. With only one league in existence, there was no way to have a postseason series between the champions of different leagues.

As a result, in 1892 the National League played a split-season to create a postseason playoff. Boston, which finished first in the second half of the season, defeated the Cleveland Spiders, the first-half winner, for the National League championship. The split season was dropped and no playoffs were held in 1893. But in 1894, a postseason championship series was resumed. Named the Temple Cup after the trophy donated by Pittsburgh sportsman William C. Temple, the series matched the first- and second-place teams from the regular season. The Baltimore Orioles finished first in 1894, three games ahead of the second-place Giants. The runner-up Giants then surprised the regular-season champions in the Temple Cup, sweeping the series, four games to none.

Three-and-a-half months after having won yet another title, the Giants had a new owner when Andrew C. Freedman bought the financial interest of Edward Talcott, the team's managing partner. Freedman's tenure as owner marked one of the stormiest periods in the history of the Giants; it also marked the transition into its greatest period.

Freedman has been maligned by baseball historians, apparently with good reason. In his 1988 book *The Giants of the Polo Grounds*, Noel Hynd wrote:

> If one were a young business student and wanted a textbook example of how a profitable business could be run in to the ground, one might settle upon the New York Giants, under the management of Andrew C. Freedman. Andrew Freedman was a man of breathtaking arrogance, appalling miserliness, and uncompromising dishonesty. The best thing that can be said for him, in 1988, is that he's currently dead.

Donald Dewey and Nicholas Acocella, in *The Biographical History of Baseball*, add, "Even in a business noted for crooks, incompetents, misers, and paranoids, Freedman [whom the authors also describe as a 'bagman for Tammany Hall's Boss Richard Croker'] stood out on all counts."

Freedman alienated members of the New York press and had even worse relations with his managers (he had 12 different managers, including erstwhile owner John B. Day, in the eight years he controlled the team) and players. The best—or worst—example of the latter is the situation that developed with star pitcher Amos Rusie. Rusie had averaged more than 30 wins per season in his six seasons with the Giants, from 1890 through 1895, when Freedman fined Rusie $200 for unspecified training-rule violations. Rusie responded by sitting out the entire 1896 season.

Following their Temple Cup victory in 1894, the Giants finished no higher than third over the next eight seasons. From 1900 through 1902, after the National League had scaled back to eight teams, the Giants finished eighth, seventh, and eighth, respectively. Freedman had taken the Giants as low as they could go. But events were transpiring that would bring about a dramatic turnaround for the occupants of the Polo Grounds.

The most significant event was the arrival of John McGraw as manager in July of 1902. McGraw had been a member of the Baltimore Orioles team that lost to the Giants in the 1894 Temple Cup (he is one of seven from that Orioles team who are now in the Hall of Fame). The dominant team of the mid-1890s, the Orioles were known more for their methods of winning than for winning itself. The Baltimore players were proponents of strategic innovations, such as the hit-and-run. But they became better known for underhanded tactics, which included hiding extra baseballs in the tall outfield grass. John McGraw epitomized the Baltimore brand of baseball of the 1890s. Playing third base, he could be counted on to impede the progress of rival base runners. One of his tricks was grabbing the belt of a runner tagging at third base on a fly ball. Following the catch, the runner would break for the plate, only to find that McGraw had hooked his belt and delayed his start. McGraw brought the same fire to the Giants.

Although the Giants finished last in the National League in 1902, the team was setting the stage for better times. Besides the addition of McGraw, the Giants ended up with a new owner as John T. Brush purchased the team from Freedman in September of 1902. Brush had owned the Cincinnati Reds since 1891 but unloaded his holdings in that club in order to purchase the Giants. Reportedly, he had actually been the force behind the hiring of McGraw as manager, carefully remaining out of sight since he was still the owner of a rival team while he was arranging for McGraw to come to New York.

Brush was a Lamb, a member of a social organization serving the theater and entertainment business. Through his recommendation, McGraw also became a Lamb. Links between the Giants and the theater were once again established, and, in the ensuing decades, the Polo Grounds beneath Coogan's Bluff became a haven for actors and actresses, just as the Polo Grounds on 110th Street had hosted such personages during the 1880s.

But more significant than those in the stands was the team on the field that Brush and McGraw were assembling. They had an outstanding pitcher to build around: Christy Mathewson, a right-hander who would win at least 30 games each season between 1903 and 1905, going on to a career total of 373 wins.

McGraw couldn't get the Giants out of the cellar in 1902, but he did help the team rise to second place in 1903. The following year, the Giants won 106 games to capture their first National League pennant since 1889.

The American League (now in its fourth season as a major league) produced an outstanding pennant race in 1904, with Boston narrowly edging out the New York Highlanders (who later became the Yankees) for the flag. It was the second straight league title for Boston, which had beat Pittsburgh, champions of the National League, in a postseason championship series the previous year. Although the 1903 event was the first of the modern-day World Series, it would not be repeated in 1904 because Brush, the owner of the National League champions, refused to acknowledge the American League as an equal and declared that his team was required to "submit its championship honors to a contest with a victorious club in a minor league."

Brush was harshly criticized for his stance and, as a result, led the way in drafting a format for a regular postseason meeting between the champions of the American and National leagues. The first official World Series was played in 1905, and the Giants—repeating as pennant winners in the National League—played in it against Connie Mack's Philadelphia Athletics.

It was a series for the pitchers, with one in particular standing out. New York took the first game, 3–0, behind a four-hitter by Mathewson. Charles "Chief" Bender, the great right-hander for Philadelphia, matched the feat with a four-hitter and 3–0 victory in Game 2. Mathewson came back, on only two days rest, to pitch another shutout in Game 3, a 9–0 Giants win. Matty's teammate, Joe "Iron Man" McGinnity, followed with a 1–0 win in the fourth game to put New York within a game of the world title.

For the fifth game of the series, at the Polo Grounds, McGraw went with his ace again, even though this time Mathewson would be working with only a day's rest between starts. He was up to the task, though, outdueling Bender of the Athletics to win the game, 2–0. All five games were shutouts, with three of them completed by one pitcher. Thanks to the dominance of Christy Mathewson, the Giants were on top again, and the Polo Grounds was the capital of the baseball world.

The Polo Grounds was a cynosure for reasons beyond the team that occupied it. A couple of sports staples—hot dogs and the song "Take Me Out to the Ball Game"—have connections with the stadium as well. Harry Mozley Stevens, the chief concessionaire at the Polo Grounds, came across the idea for a sausage sandwich while searching for a new food to offer fans. He instructed his vendors to purchase wursts known as dachshund sausages; after wrapping the meat in Vienna bread, Stevens sent his vendors through the stands hollering, "Get your dachshund sausages while they're red hot!" The name was a bit of a mouthful and soon enough was shorted to "hot dog." It wasn't long before hot dogs became standard at other ballparks.

Peanuts and Cracker Jack are other snack items associated with baseball games, thanks in part to their inclusion in the lyrics of "Take Me Out to the Ball Game," composed in 1908 by Jack Norworth, who was inspired by the sight of an advertisement for baseball at the Polo Grounds in a New York subway car. While the chorus is the most familiar part of the song, its verses center on a baseball-mad lass named Katie Casey. According to John W. Ripley's 1983 article in *American Heritage* magazine, the song's success was due to the publisher's decision to plug the tune nationwide with song slides. "The thriving nickelodeons had added illustrated song acts to their one- and two-reelers," wrote Ripley, "and the song-slide treatment had boosted several tunes into hits." The slides for "Take Me Out to the Ball Game,"which depicted an afternoon in the life of Katie Casey, used the Polo Grounds as a backdrop.

The Polo Grounds were in many ways associated with greatness. During John McGraw's reign, the stadium was also the scene of much tumult. A strange situation unfolded at the stadium in August of 1906. In a Tuesday, August 7, game between New York and Chicago, McGraw and Giants third baseman Art Devlin were ejected from the game by umpire James Johnstone. The next day, when Johnstone arrived to umpire the Cubs-Giants game, he found himself barred from the Polo Grounds. When Bob Emslie, Johnstone's umpiring partner, arrived at the Polo Grounds and learned the news about his associate, he immediately left.

With no actual umpires on hand, McGraw asked one of his utility players, Sammy Strang, to make the calls. It wasn't unusual for players to assume such a fill-in role in the early part of the century, but, on this occasion, the Cubs would have none of it. Carrying their bats, the Cubs made a dash across the field for the clubhouse in center field, signaling to the fans there would be no game that day. Strang, the closest thing to an umpire left in the stadium, declared a forfeit victory for the Giants because of the Cubs' refusal to play. Of course, the National League would stand for no such fiasco. League president Harry Pulliam announced that the victory was awarded to Chicago, not New York.

Another forfeit occurred in the opening game of the 1907 season at the Polo Grounds. This time it was the crowd, not the Giants management, that was out of control. One of the problems was the decision of the New York police commissioner to strictly enforce an ordinance that forbade the policing of private grounds with the city force and thus required the Giants to provide their own security. When the game started, only two actual police officers—both were assigned to the police ambulance and refused entreaties to assist with crowd control—were on hand.

The fans remained orderly enough on their own until the eighth inning. With the Giants down by three runs, some decided to leave the game early. The problem was that they chose to leave by their usual route—across the playing field and out a gate beyond center field. Such a means of exit was common in many ballparks, but normally not until after the game had ended.

As the first throng ambled across the playing area, umpire Bill Klem urged them to hurry along so as to not delay the game. But the crowd, apparently having given up hope of a Giant comeback and seeking other ways of amusing themselves, sided with the stragglers, jeering Klem for his attempts at clearing the field. In the ninth inning, a larger group decided to defy the umpire's authority again, and approximately 1,000 men and boys scaled the fences surrounding the playing area and rushed onto the field. The players joined umpire Klem in pleading with the fans to return to their seats or leave the stadium, but all this did was encourage others to join the group on the field. Many who remained in their seats began hurling their seat cushions onto the field. With a near-riot breaking out, Klem had no choice but to award a victory to the visiting Philadelphia team.

These bizarre scenes, however, were only a prelude to what would happen at the Polo Grounds in the final weeks of the 1908 season. A three-way race for the National League pennant was winding down, with both the Giants and the Pittsburgh Pirates trying to stymie the Chicago Cubs in their drive for a third-consecutive league title. The Cubs were led by player-manager Frank Chance, who, at first base, anchored the famous double-play combination that included shortstop Joe Tinker and second baseman Johnny Evers. Leading the mound corps for Chicago was right-hander Mordecai Brown, whose nickname of "Three-Fingered" was the result of a childhood accident with a corn grinder; this unfortunate accident, however, is what led to Brown's greatness as a pitcher, since he could achieve quite a spin and a greater break on his pitches by releasing the ball off the stub of his forefinger. The Pirates lineup also included Honus Wagner, by far the greatest shortstop of the period, who was on his way to leading the National League in batting average for the sixth time and in stolen bases for the fifth time. Behind player-manager Fred Clarke, Pittsburgh was seeking its first pennant since 1903.

It was the custom of the period for players to get to their dressing rooms as quickly as possible after a game, sometimes to avoid the rush of fans exiting across the playing area. If a game ended with a run being scored in the last of the ninth or extra innings, other base runners would immediately leave the diamond, sometimes not bothering even to touch the ensuing bases. Normally, the team in the field ignored such transgressions—until September of 1908.

The Cubs and Pirates were locked in a scoreless game in Pittsburgh on Friday, September 4. In the last of the tenth, Pittsburgh loaded the bases with two out off Three-Fingered Brown. Owen Wilson then drove a single into center to bring Clarke home with the winning run. Warren Gill, the Pirate runner on first base, pulled up short of second base and headed toward his team's dressing room. Crafty Johnny Evers, however, was not going to allow the normal courtesy of excusing such an omission. He called for the ball from the outfield and stepped on second, claiming a force out to end the inning and thus wipe out Clarke's run. Unfortunately for Evers, umpire Hank O'Day had already departed, joining the others in a hasty exit, and was in no position to call the runner out. The Cubs protested the game to the league office but had little hope of having it upheld. They were right. Clarke's run stood, and the Pirates won the game, 1–0.

Even though Evers and the Cubs were not successful in their attempt in Pittsburgh, they weren't averse to trying again—and a similar opportunity presented itself fewer than three weeks later. On Wednesday, September 23, the Cubs and Giants—in a virtual tie for first place—were tied 1–1 in the last of the ninth at the Polo Grounds. Hank O'Day was again umpiring. The Giants had Moose McCormick on third and rookie Fred Merkle on first with two out when Al Bridwell singled to center, bringing in McCormick with the winning run—or so it appeared. Merkle headed for the clubhouse without bothering to touch second. Chicago, presented with another opportunity to complete an inning-ending force play that would wipe out the run, intended to do so. And this time, umpire O'Day held his ground.

A mad scene took place as infielders Chance and Evers attempted to get the ball thrown in from the outfield. With fans swarming onto the field, and with some of the Giants catching wind of what the Cubs were up to and trying to stop them, it is unclear exactly what happened and when. But somehow, Evers got hold of a ball (whether it was the same ball Bridwell hit is anybody's guess) and stepped on second base, claiming a force out. O'Day withheld his ruling until he was in the safety of his dressing room. Once there, however, he sided with the Cubs, calling Merkle out. With fans still swarming on the field, and with darkness setting in, it was too late to resume play, so the game ended as a 1–1 tie.

The *New York Times* wasn't shy about placing the blame in its edition the next day: "Censurable stupidity on the part of player Merkle in yesterday's game at the Polo Grounds between the Giants and Chicagos placed the New York team's chances of winning the pennant in jeopardy. His unusual conduct in the final inning of a great game perhaps deprived New York of a victory that would have been unquestionable had he not committed a breach in baseball play that resulted in Umpire O'Day declaring the game a tie."

Others were kinder, including Fred Snodgrass, another rookie who had spent most of the season warming the bench with Merkle. (Merkle had received his only starting assignment of the season in the fateful game.) Years later, Snodgrass recalled the incident for Lawrence S. Ritter in *The Glory of Their Times:*

> As soon as a game was over at the Polo Grounds, any game, all of us fellows who were sitting on the bench were in the habit, when the last out was made, of jumping up and running like the dickens for our clubhouse, which was out beyond right-center field. We wanted to get there before the crowd could get on the field. In those days, as soon as a game ended at the Polo Grounds the ushers would open the gates from the stands to the field, and the people would all pour out and rush at you. Of course, all they wanted to do was touch you, or congratulate you, or maybe cuss you out a bit. But, because of that, as soon as a game was over we bench warmers all made it a practice to sprint from the bench to the clubhouse as fast as we could. And that was precisely the reason why Fred Merkle got into that awful jam. He was so used to sitting on the bench all during the game, and then at the end of the game jumping up with the rest of us and taking off as fast as he could for the clubhouse, that on this particular day he did it by force of habit and never gave it a second thought.

History, however, hasn't been as kind as Snodgrass, and ever since the play has been known as "Merkle's Boner." (For several years after the incident, newspapers were known to use the term "Merkleized" to refer to a baserunning gaffe.) Although the Giants contended that McCormick's run should be counted and the game awarded to them, National League President Pulliam backed his umpire's decision. It wasn't the end of the controversy, however, which continued over the next two weeks as the Giants, Cubs, and Pirates battled through the remainder of the schedule.

On Sunday, October 4, the Cubs and Pirates met in Chicago in what was the last scheduled game of the regular season for both teams. Pittsburgh, with a win-loss record of 98–55, was in first place by a half-game over the Cubs. The idle Giants (Sunday ball still being outlawed in New York) were in third place with a record of 95–55, and they were getting ready to begin a three-game series against Boston to conclude their schedule.

More than 30,000 turned out in Chicago to see the game against the Pirates. An even greater crowd showed up in downtown Pittsburgh, with the fans assembling outside the windows of newspaper offices so they could receive immediate updates on the game from employees of the newspapers, who would be getting a play-by-play account via telegraph wires and relaying the news on to the fans through megaphones.

A similar event took place in New York, although it was at the Polo Grounds, where more than 5,000 fans paid 25 cents each to witness a play-by-play reproduction of the Chicago-Pittsburgh game. The reproduction was done on boards, about 20 feet wide and 15 feet high, with the diamond and playing field reproduced with incandescent lights to indicate the players on the field and at bat. Other lights were arranged in such a manner to "show strikes, called balls, fouls, flies, and practically every play possible on the diamond." As word of what had transpired in Chicago reached officials in the

Polo Grounds, the results were posted. (This system had also been used at Madison Square Garden to bring fans immediate updates on recent Giant games while the team was on a road trip; more than 2,000 fans had come to the Garden on Sunday, September 6, to follow a Cubs-Pirates doubleheader in Pittsburgh.) The spectators at the Polo Grounds for the October 4 reproduction included players from the New York and Boston teams, waiting to start their series the next day.

Behind Three-Fingered Brown, the Cubs beat the Pirates, 5–2, to move into first place. The Chicago victory appeared to end any Pittsburgh hopes of a pennant, since the Cubs had the same number of wins as the Pirates but one fewer loss. (At the time, uncompleted schedules that resulted from tied or rained-out games weren't played out—even if the games had a bearing on first place.)

The Giants still had a shot at catching the Cubs. Three wins over Boston would put New York and Chicago into a first-place tie and require a playoff game between the two to determine the National League champion. In the midst of the New York-Boston series, however, the National League ruled that the September 23 tie game between the Giants and Cubs would have to be replayed on Thursday, October 8. This news now gave Pittsburgh another chance at first place, since a Giant win over the Cubs in the replayed game would drop Chicago back into a tie with the Pirates (but only if New York did not first win all its games versus Boston).

The possibility actually existed for a three-way tie for the pennant (if the Giants won two of three from Boston, then beat Chicago in the replayed game). However, New York swept its series with Boston, once again eliminating Pittsburgh from the race and giving the Giants and Cubs similar records of 98 wins and 55 losses. It meant the replay of the tie game would decide the pennant and determine which team—Chicago or New York—would advance to the World Series.

Perhaps never before had there been such interest in seeing a baseball game. "It is impossible to estimate just how many people will witness the game," reported the *New York Times* the morning of the game. "After the gates are closed there will probably be 35,000 persons on the grounds, the Viaduct will be packed, and the Speedway [then the name of Harlem River Drive], together with Coogan's Bluff, will be lined with a black mass of humanity. . . . The average fan will go to almost any length to hear the cry, 'Play Ball!' But to-day, when the Giants play off the pennant-deciding tie game with the Chicagos, this feeling will be intensified a hundredfold."

The Giants management even had watchmen on patrol the previous evening to prevent the bleachers from filling up overnight. The police also anticipated the need for crowd control for the event, but no one—not the team, not the newspapers, not the police department—came close to predicting the size of the throng that came for the game, nor the determination of those in the crowd to see it.

Many showed up in the middle of the night and staked out spots in line along Eighth Avenue. Through the morning, the crowd outside the stadium built. Finally at 11:00—four hours before the scheduled start of the game—the gates were opened and the masses flooded in. A new section of grandstand, only partially completed, was opened for the first time and was filled quickly, as was every other unreserved seat in the stadium. Fans were then sent to areas on the playing field in foul territory, and soon all space allotted for this purpose was filled.

Those with tickets for reserved seats arrived later, not anticipating that they would have to fight for access to their seats. But they learned otherwise as police, some on horseback, and Giant management worked furiously to keep the growing mob outside the stadium under control. At 1:00 the gates were closed and fans, with or without tickets, were denied entry. Even newspaper reporters with credentials were turned back. Family members of the team—including the wives of manager John McGraw, pitcher Christy Mathewson, and catcher Roger Bresnahan—were admitted, but only after they found themselves serving as the unwilling center of a flying wedge that included others aiming for the gate that was briefly opened to accommodate the wives.

Some went home, but others tried alternative means of entry, which included scaling fences topped with barbed wire, burrowing under the fences, and, at one point on the south side of the stadium, burning the fence down. Most of the fans who couldn't get in were content to stake out any high spot in the vicinity. Taking places on the lawn of the Jumel Mansion on 160th Street; curling around Coogan's Bluff, lining the 155th Street viaduct; and occupying telegraph poles, stairs, and fence tops along Eighth Avenue; fans vied for any vantage point that offered a glimpse of the field or even just the outside of the stadium. "Never before in the history of the game have there been so many people to see a game who didn't see it," wrote W. J. Lampton in his account for the *New York Times*.

No matter how well they could see the contest itself, fans could sense what was happening. In the last of the first inning, "Turkey Mike" Donlin doubled home Fred Tenney to give the Giants a 1–0 lead. Fans inside and out cheered, including a man named Henry McBride, who was occupying a pillar on the elevated station beyond the center-field fence. So vociferously did

McBride celebrate that he lost his balance and somersaulted through the air to his death on the cobblestones 25 feet below. McBride's vacated spot on the pillar was quickly filled.

Inside the stadium, the Giants threatened to add to their lead, but Chicago manager Frank Chance found a way to quell the rally. He replaced starter Jack Pfiester with his ace, Three-Fingered Brown. Brown put out the fire and held the Giants without another tally until the seventh inning. By this time, the Cubs had managed to reach the mighty Mathewson for four runs, enough to allow them to hold on for a 4–2 victory and the National League pennant.

Depending upon the accuracy of estimates provided by the various New York newspapers, anywhere from 80,000 to 100,000 fans showed up and attempted—successfully or otherwise—to see the game. The grandstand that opened for the first time this day was part of an outgoing expansion of the Polo Grounds that coincided with the revival of the Giants under John McGraw. Since 1902, the Giants had gradually increased their seating capacity, accelerating efforts during the great pennant race of 1908.

At the time McGraw was hired in 1902, the stadium had 5,500 grandstand seats and bleachers that accommodated 5,000 more. According to John T. Brush, in an article he wrote years later for *Baseball Magazine* titled "The Evolution of the Baseball Grandstand":

> The first extension of seats removed old "Burkville" [a section of outfield seats named for the Irish immigrant fans who sat there] and added 3,000 bleacher seats in left field. The next improvement added 2,000 bleacher seats in right field and the present clubhouse. Then followed an extension of 150 feet added to the south end of the grandstand. This being insufficient, the year following 150 feet were added to the north end and the bleacher seats increased to over 11,000. The last extension added 176 feet to the south end of the grandstand and increased the bleacher capacity to over 13,000.

In 1910, another feature was added with the construction of a wooden approach from the Speedway on Coogan's Bluff to the second level of the grandstand. By this time, the wooden structure extended the entire distance around the field. The expansion also meant the end of carriages being able to park on the running track beyond the rope fence that ran across center field. Before long, however, there would be an even greater loss.

The Giants opened the 1911 season at the Polo Grounds against the Philadelphia Phillies. Although they had an outstanding team with high hopes of getting to the World Series, the Giants were defeated in their first two games. In the latter, on Thursday, April 13, Philadelphia center fielder Dode Paskert helped preserve his team's victory with one of the most remarkable catches ever seen at the Polo Grounds, according to the *New York Times*, robbing Fred Snodgrass of an extra-base hit and possibly a home run on a long drive to left-center field. "With the crack of the bat Paskert turned around and ran toward the fence," reported the *Times:*

> His chances of reaching that ball were worth about a nickel. On, on Paskert galloped. His right arm was stretched as far into the air as it would go, and he made a desperate leap, as if leaving the earth forevermore. The ball just about met his finger tips. The bare right hand squeezed the bulb and Paskert kept right on running. Everybody in the stands thought the ball had rolled to the fence and Snodgrass kept on pushing around the bases. The umpires were dumbfounded and didn't know what had happened. Paskert came running in and when he reached the diamond, he tossed the ball into the air from the hand where it had stuck.

Another inning remained, but Paskert's gem effectively ended the Giants' comeback hopes for the game. Even though no one in the stadium knew it at the time, the catch provided an exclamation point to the stormy history of Polo Grounds III.

Shortly after midnight on Friday, April 14, a fire began in the lower timbers of the grandstand. A brisk wind from the southeast swept the fire over the grounds and with an hour, most of the structure was ablaze with flames leaping nearly 100 feet in the air. The first alarm was issued at 12:40, but by this time the fire had swept around the entire circle of grandstand seats and was spreading to the storage yards of the elevated lines that adjoined the stadium on the north.

With most of the stadium already lost, firefighters turned their attention to saving the storage yards of the elevated, where they were joined by railroad workers who had formed bucket squads. By 2:00 A.M. the fire was under control. All that remained of the Polo Grounds were some bleachers in left field and the clubhouse/office building at the Eighth Avenue end, which were saved because they were separated by a gap from the portions of the stadium that were on fire.

Events within the Polo Grounds had attracted many spectators over the past decades. So did the conflagration that put an end to the stadium. Harlem residents, seeking the flicker out of their windows, headed for the site on foot and via the elevated lines. Many who chose the latter route found themselves stranded. Firefighters were operating from the 155th Street platform, and the danger of electrocution necessitated shutting down the power on the lines. Meanwhile, taxi cabs and private automobiles were bringing in more of the morbid every minute, and eventually the throng on the hillside above the grounds was spread out for blocks in all directions. "Coogan's Bluff was a sea of eager faces, lit up by the flames," reported the *New York Times*.

One face in the crowd that undoubtedly did not contain an eager expression belonged to John McGraw, who arrived at the scene soon after the fire broke out and watched it spread throughout the stands.

The cause of the fire was never pinpointed. The custodian of the grounds, a retired fire captain named John F. Higgins, declared that an incendiary had been used. "I don't like to say that anyone deliberately set fire to the Polo Grounds, but there is no other explanation," he told the fire marshal. But the fire department discounted the claim and rendered the official opinion that a smoldering fire among dried peanut shells and other debris, fanned by the wind, was responsible for the blaze.

A young sportswriter named Fred Lieb, who was later to become a legend, was breaking into the profession in 1911, arriving just in time to cover the final games at the stadium. He was taken by the late-inning catch made by Dode Paskert in the last game, and years later reflected in his memoirs on both the play and the fire that followed hours later: "Reporters who were there liked to call the official account of the fire's origin nonsense: it was Paskert's electrifying and sizzling catch, they said, that sparked the Polo Grounds holocaust."

CHAPTER SIX

A Grand New Stadium

BUT A MORE IMMEDIATE CONCERN WAS WHERE THE GIANTS WOULD PLAY their home games while plans were developed and implemented for a new stadium.

Tragedy has a way of bringing enemies together. Such was the case with the burning of the Polo Grounds, after which the Giants received offers of help from unlikely sources. One was from Brooklyn owner Charles Ebbets, inviting the Giants to share his stadium. Because of their closeness, a special enmity had developed between the New York and Brooklyn teams, establishing a rivalry that continued even after the Giants and Dodgers moved to California.

Even more surprising than the kindness of Ebbets was a similar offer from Frank Farrell, owner of the New York Highlanders of the American League. Barely 10 years before, the Giants management had tried to prevent the upstart American League from moving a team into New York and still deeply resented the presence of the Highlanders.

But the Giants, with their stadium in ashes, were in no position to harbor grudges. They transferred their home games to the Highlanders' stadium, Hilltop Park, located on the highest point of land on Manhattan Island, on a rock pile over looking the Hudson River, not far from the charred remains of the Polo Grounds.

Meanwhile, the team directors began dealing with the questions regarding the construction of a new facility. John T. Brush had known that the wooden structure would not last indefinitely, but he had been hesitant to dismantle it and erect a stadium with more durable materials because of the lack of a long-term lease on the property. The current lease with the Coogan estate, signed the year before, was for only 10 years. But it was also apparent that any new stadium would have to be of the latest design, which consisted of steel and concrete.

Fires in wooden stadiums were not uncommon. Only a few weeks before the destruction of the Polo Grounds, the wooden stadium used by the Washington Senators in the American League had burned down. Fortunately, the damage in these blazes was limited to property, but the New York building commissioner said had the Polo Grounds fire occurred while a game was in progress, it was probable that lives would have been lost.

The city's Board of Coroners went further in urging the Giants to use different materials in a new stadium. A statement issued by the board read: "We issue a warning to the owners of the grounds and also to the officials of the New York Baseball Club that in case the stands are rebuilt of anything but fireproof material and there is the loss of life, we are going to hold these owners and the New York baseball officials without bail. We, the Coroners, say the public must be protected."

John Brush didn't argue. He was determined to build a new stadium with the latest in materials and design. One poignant account has Brush, in a wheelchair (he suffered from locomotor ataxia), visiting the smoldering ruins of the Polo Grounds with his wife, Elsie, and saying: "I want to build a concrete stand—the finest thing that can be constructed. It will mean economy for a time. Are you willing to stand by me?" Elsie reportedly acquiesced, and Brush was underway with his plans for a massive new facility.

Whether this touching version is apocryphal, it is clear that Brush had Osborn Engineering Company—a Cleveland firm that made its mark as the designing and structural engineers in many stadiums built in the first quarter of the twentieth century—in town within days of the fire, starting plans for a stadium to be built on the same site as the previous one, even though he still had the issue of a long-term lease to consider. Within two weeks, however, that matter had been resolved as the Giants agreed to a 25-year lease with the Coogan estate.

This out of the way, plans progressed quickly for the building of the new stadium, which was to be patterned after the new wave of recently opened or remodeled ballparks that had steel and reinforced concrete as their primary building materials, a list that included Forbes Field in Pittsburgh, League Park in Cleveland, Shibe Park in Philadelphia, and Comiskey Park in

Chicago. This period—known as the era of classic stadiums—continued for another dozen years. "These palaces signaled the growing prominence of baseball," wrote Phil Lowry of the classic ballparks in *Green Cathedrals.*

Although other teams were constructing impressive edifices, John Brush had ambitions for a stadium for the Giants that would surpass all others in terms of size, structure, and design. His wishes were carried out. The substructure of the new stadium consisted of spread, reinforced concrete piers rising to the level of the first tier of seats. This tier was built of reinforced concrete in the form of a great slab supported by girders across the piers. Construction above the first tier was open steel framing with the upper deck and roof cantilevered out.

Although described as "utilitarian" by Henry B. Herts—the architectural designer of numerous buildings in New York, including many theaters—the stadium contained many visually appealing elements. The facade of the upper deck was faced with a decorative frieze that depicted a series of allegorical treatments in bas-relief, while the facade of the roof was adorned with the insignia of all National League teams. "The design at the balcony level is a repeated motif," explained Herts in an article written for *Architecture and Building* magazine in 1912, "while that at the roof level contains a series of eight shields repeated in successive panels." The box seats were designed upon the lines of the royal boxes of the Colosseum in Rome, with pylons flanking the horseshoe-shaped grandstand on both ends. The aisle seats had figural iron scrollwork with the Giants' "NY" emblem.

Brush planned to depart from the nomenclature traditionally used for the home of the Giants; the new facility, to reflect his own contribution, would be known as Brush Stadium. Fans and news reporters had other ideas, though, and the name Polo Grounds persevered. As Lawrence S. Ritter said of the rebuilt structure in his book *Lost Ballparks*, "Polo Grounds it had been and Polo Grounds it would remain."

Construction in steel and concrete began on May 10, 1911, and by late June, fewer than 11 weeks after the wooden Polo Grounds had burned, the new stadium was ready for baseball. The double-decked grandstand retained the horseshoe configuration of its predecessor although it was built upon much larger lines, rising higher and extending back further, and consisted entirely of steel and reinforced concrete. The only wood used anywhere in the stadium was found in the movable folding opera chairs in the semicircle in back of the diamond and in the roof sheathing.

As before, the main entrance was on Eighth Avenue, accessible via the Eighth Avenue surface lines. Along the Harlem River Speedway, at the rear of the stadium (behind home plate), was a large auxiliary entrance with 10-foot-wide inclines leading to runways to both the upper and lower decks. "The most convenient automobile or carriage entrance is on the Speedway, opposite 157th Street. When taking the Subway, stop at 157th Street Station, passing north to 158th Street, and then east down the Brush Stairway, built by the New York Base Ball Club, to the new Speedway entrance," were the instructions provided in *Scenes on the Polo Grounds*, a commemorative booklet issued by the New York Giants.

"Upon the ruins of the old historic stand, with its contour and general plan of entrance and exit unchanged—the old being by far the best arranged grandstand in the country—there rises majestic, 100 feet above the ground and more than a thousand feet in length, the latest contribution to the comfort and convenience of the baseball fan," wrote John T. Brush in "The Evolution of the Baseball Grandstand" in the April 1912 issue of *Baseball Magazine*. In an earlier issue of the magazine, John Foster had written:

> Indeed there is everything at the Polo Grounds that may be found at a first-class theatre. . . . There is another effect about the new stadium which no theatre could ever have. This feature is its massive beauty. Take it away from the background of the lofty rocky bluff behind it, and stretch it out on a plain, and it would command the same air of respect which is held by the pyramids built in all their silent grandeur on the shifting sands of the desert.

Still another *Baseball Magazine* writer, Allan Sangree, called the rebuilt Polo Grounds "the mightiest temple ever erected to the goddess of sport and the crowning achievement among notable structures devoted to baseball."

Only 16,000 seats—all in the lower deck—were available for occupancy on Wednesday, June 28, 1911, but it was enough to bring the Giants into their new home on the old lot in Coogan's Hollow. Christy Mathewson was on the mound for the Giants in first game at Polo Grounds IV and shut out Boston, 3–0. "Laughing Larry" Doyle, the New York second baseman often remembered for his exuberant quote, "It's great to be young and a Giant," broke up the scoreless duel in the sixth inning with a home run into the right-field stands.

Work continued on the stadium's superstructure through the rest of the season. It was becoming apparent that the remainder of the seats would be needed come fall, because the Giants were in the race for the pennant. They did come out on top in the National League, and the Polo Grounds by this time could hold 34,000 fans for the 1911 World Series against the Philadelphia Athletics. The Giants had been successful in every previous post-season championship series in which they had participated. This time, however, their streak came to an end as the Athletics won the series, four games to two. The Giants made it three pennants—and three World Series losses—in a row as they were beaten by the Boston Red Sox in 1912 and again by the Philadelphia Athletics in 1913. (Still another World Series loss came at the hands of the Chicago White Sox in 1917.)

Three stadiums before had been known as the Polo Grounds, but the one that opened in 1911 would last twice as long as the other three combined. It would carry the Giants through the golden years of its history and then serve as the home of a new team after the Giants abandoned New York for the West Coast. And, for 10 years in its early going, the Polo Grounds served as the home of the New York American League team in addition to the Giants. The New York Highlanders (by this time about to make the transformation to "Yankees" as their exclusive nickname) had hoped to build a new ballpark in the northern reaches of Manhattan to replace the decrepit Hilltop Park. Lowry has said that the Yankees even considered a floating ballpark in the Harlem River. However, neither proposition worked out, and in 1913 the Yankees looked at sharing the Polo Grounds with the Giants, hoping the National Leaguers would return the favor of hospitality that had been extended to them two years before. The Giants were amenable to letting the Yankees sign a 10-year lease to use the Polo Grounds. After all, it wasn't as though the Giants felt threatened by their tenants; the Yankees were among the American League doormats and didn't appear likely to steal the spotlight from the Giants.

Shoeless Joe Jackson of Cleveland became the first player to hit a home run over the roof in right field in Polo Grounds IV on Wednesday, June 4, 1913. His drive, off the Yankees' Russ Ford, passed out of sight just inside the foul pole, landed on the roof, and bounded into the vacant lot to the south that was still known as Manhattan Field.

It was more than six years before the feat was topped. This time, the home run was significant for more than its distance. It was hit by Babe Ruth, and it was Ruth's twenty-eighth home run of the year, setting a new major league single-season record. Ruth hit it not for—but against—the Yankees, the team he would become most closely associated with, because on Wednesday, September 24, 1919, Ruth was still a member of the Boston Red Sox. He was spending his first year as a full-time outfielder, after having been one of the top left-handed pitchers in baseball in the preceding seasons. The long homer, which tied the game in the ninth inning, cleared the entire structure without even bouncing off the roof, as Jackson's 1913 smash had.

The decade of 1911 to 1920 had begun for the Giants with the loss of their stadium. But the new one that rose on the same site had more than its share of memorable moments—some odd, some outlandish—in its first 10 years. One of the strangest came near the end of the 1911 season. The story of Charles Victor "Victory" Faust actually began in late July, when the Giants were in St. Louis, about to start a series against the Cardinals. With his team in third place, John McGraw had hopes of returning to the World Series that year for the first time since 1905. Thus, he was in an amenable mood when approached by Faust (who claimed his middle name was "Victory") with an offer to help the Giants. Based on advice he had recently received from a fortune-teller, Faust had left his home in Kansas, intent on finding fame as a pitcher with a New York Giants.

McGraw invited the lanky Kansan to the ballpark for a chance to show his stuff. Clad in a dark suit and a derby, Faust took the mound and—with his long arms gyrating in a windup resembling an out-of-control windmill—delivered a number of pitches, enough to show that he was eminently unqualified for such a profession. McGraw then suggested he take a turn with the bat. "Word was quickly passed around to the fellows who were shagging balls in the infield," according to Fred Snodgrass in *The Glory of Their Times*. "Charlie Faust dribbled one down to the shortstop who juggled it a minute as Charlie was turning first, and then they deliberately slid him into second, slid him into third, and slid him into home, all in his best Sunday suit—to the obvious enjoyment of everyone."

It was clear that Charley Faust would be of little help to the Giants with either his pitching or hitting, but the superstitious McGraw wondered if the man wouldn't serve as a mascot who would bring good luck to the team. Faust was thus invited to spend most of the rest of the 1911 season with the Giants, and was even issued a uniform. McGraw often had him warm up before and during a game, as if he were actually going to get the chance to pitch. Whatever charms he brought to the Giants seemed to be working as the team moved into first place and pulled away from the rest of the pack.

In October, with the pennant assured and the Giants playing out the rest of their National League schedule, McGraw decided to reward Faust for his efforts by actually inserting him into a game. Only about 1,000 fans turned out on a cold Saturday, October 7, to see the Giants play Boston at the Polo Grounds. As usual, Faust spent the afternoon warming up in the bullpen. But in the ninth, he was summoned by McGraw and received a huge ovation from the small gathering as he trotted in toward the mound. The Giants were trailing, 4–2, in a game that meant absolutely nothing to them, and McGraw was giving Faust his chance to pitch for real. Employing his peculiar windup, Faust faced four batters and gave up one run. In the last of the ninth, he was on deck with two out. If New York catcher Grover Hartley could keep the inning going, Faust would get a chance to hit, something the fans were staying in their seats to see. However, Hartley made the third out of the inning to end the game. Rather than leave the field, though, the Boston players signaled for Faust to take his spot in the batter's box. He hit a weak grounder back to pitcher Lefty Tyler, who intentionally fired the ball wildly to first base. Alive on the bases, Charley headed for second and ran on as Boston players continued to heave the ball about wildly. Faust hustled into third with a long slide through the mud and then headed for home, as the ball had been overthrown again. This time, however, the throw to the catcher was true, and Faust was tagged out at the plate. It was a scene that resembled his initial tryout with the Giants in St. Louis, except that this time Faust was actually wearing a baseball uniform.

The Giants closed out their 1911 regular season five days later with a doubleheader against Brooklyn. In the second game, Faust pitched another inning and then had the chance to bat in the bottom of that inning. He reached base after being hit on the wrist with a pitch, then stole second and third before coming home after tagging up on a fly ball. Those were Faust's only two official appearances in a major league game.

Of course, what was really expected of Faust was good luck, but his stock in that department went down when the Giants were defeated by the Philadelphia Athletics in the 1911 World Series. Disillusioned and made aware that he was no longer welcome, Faust eventually left the Giants. He ended up in a hospital for the insane in Fort Steilacoom, Washington, and in June of 1915 died of pulmonary tuberculosis at the age of 34.

With or without the help of Charles Victor(y) Faust, winning streaks—individual and team—were another source of headlines for the Giants around this time. In 1912, New York southpaw Rube Marquard won his first 19 games of the season, which tied the record for consecutive victories in a single season that had been set by Tim Keefe of the Giants in 1888. It also put him within a win of the overall record for consecutive wins, which had been set by John Luby of Chicago in 1890–91.

Marquard's nineteenth win of the season came in the first game of a doubleheader at the Polo Grounds on Wednesday, July 3, as he outdueled Brooklyn's Nap Rucker for a 2–1 win. The Giants won the second game of the doubleheader, giving them 16 straight victories. However, this was the end of the streak for both New York and Marquard. The Giants were swept in a doubleheader by Brooklyn the next day, and Marquard, in his next start, was roughed up in Chicago, losing to the Cubs by a score of 7–2.

Four years later, the Giants enjoyed a pair of long winning streaks. After starting the 1916 season with only two wins in their first 15 games, New York reeled off 17 wins in a row, all of them on the road. (In the days when trains were the primary method of travel, it wasn't unusual for a team to be on the road, or at home, for an extended period.) The streak pulled New York out of the cellar and lifted the team into second place. However, over the next three months, the Giants slipped back in the standings and were in fourth place with a record of 59–62 after losing to Brooklyn on Wednesday, September 6. The next day, approximately 5,000 fans came to the Polo Grounds, not a bad crowd considering the mediocrity of the team along with the fact that it was the first day of a streetcar strike in New York (although the subways and elevated lines were continuing to operate). Those who turned out were treated to a fine performance by Ferdie Schupp, who allowed Brooklyn only two hits in leading New York to a 4–1 win. The next day, the Giants jumped on Philadelphia's Grover Cleveland Alexander, who had 27 wins coming into the game, for a 9–3 victory. New York won three more games before the Phillies left town, then turned their attention to Cincinnati. This series provided a homecoming for Christy Mathewson, the greatest pitcher in team history, who was now managing the Reds. (Mathewson had started the season with New York and had two victories in the Giants' May winning streak, including a 3–0 win over Boston for the team's seventeenth straight win.) The Polo Grounds fans gave Matty a warm reception but the Giants refused to do the same, chasing Cincinnati out with four wins over the Reds.

New York increased its winning streak to 12 games before ending up in a 1–1 tie against the Pirates in a game stopped by rain after eight innings. While technically the tie interrupted the string of victories, the Giants were still considered to be in the midst of a streak as they continued piling up the wins at the Polo Grounds.

But the streak was on the verge of ending on Wednesday, September 27, when St. Louis held a 2–0 lead with two out in the last of the ninth. But Buck Herzog tripled off the right-field fence, driving in two runs to tie the score, and the Giants eventually won in extra innings, giving them 23 in a row. By this time, New York had set a major league record (one that still stands) for consecutive victories and won another three to bring the streak to 26 before it was finally broken. The earlier streak had been achieved entirely on the road; all 26 wins in this streak happened at the Polo Grounds. When the Giants weren't streaking in 1916, though, they were playing dismally. Except for the two massive streaks, the Giants had a record of 43–66 and finished the season in fourth place.

During this time, the Giants still weren't able to play games at the Polo Grounds on Sunday. Some of the league's western cities did permit Sunday ball, but the Giants were assured of a day off every week while at home. The prohibition in New York in the 1910s wasn't as restrictive as it had been in the 1880s, when youngsters could be arrested for playing baseball in the sandlots on Sunday. By this time, the ban applied only to charging admission to see a baseball game. Teams sometimes found creative ways to skirt the rules. In 1912, the Giants scheduled an exhibition game against the Yankees at the Polo Grounds on Sunday, April 21, as a benefit for the relief fund set up for the *Titanic*, the liner that had sunk less than a week before. Instead of selling tickets for the game, the Giants required fans to purchase a program (which, not coincidentally, cost the same amount as the usual price of a ticket). More than 14,000 fans came to the Polo Grounds that day (raising nearly $9,500 for the relief fund through their program purchases) and saw the Giants beat the Yankees, 11–2.

The Giants decided to try the gambit again in 1917. As part of a benefit for the Sixty-Ninth New York Regiment—which was about to leave for France to take part in the Great War—the Giants moved up the date of a game against the Cincinnati Reds to Sunday, August 19. The 2,100 European-bound troops marched from the armory on 25th Street and Lexington Avenue to the East River at 34th Street, where they boarded a ferry that transported them to the foot of 157th Street. From there the troops paraded to the Polo Grounds, entering through the Eighth Avenue gate, and drilled on the field. A concert took place next, followed by the first official Sunday game for the Giants within the city limits of New York (the 1912 benefit for the *Titanic* having been an exhibition game).

The event was popular with New Yorkers. More than 25,000 fans turned out for the concert and game, watching the Reds shut out the Giants, 5–0. The Giants circumvented the Sunday law by stipulating that they were charging patrons for the concert, then allowing them to watch the baseball game for free (with all proceeds turned over to war charities).

This time, though, they ran into problems as city officials sought to prosecute the two managers—Christy Mathewson of Cincinnati and John McGraw of New York—for violating the Sabbath under Section 2145 of the Penal Code. (There is irony in Mathewson being prosecuted on this charge. As a player, Mathewson had never pitched on Sunday, honoring a promise he had made to his mother.)

Mathewson and McGraw were called to court two days after the game, but the charges against them were quickly dismissed by Magistrate Francis X.

"Frank" McQuade, who actually praised those involved in the Sunday game for their altruism. "Instead of being summoned to answer a charge of this kind," McQuade declared, "Mr. McGraw and Mr. Mathewson ought to receive a public vote of the highest commendation for lending their service gratis to this patriotic cause." McQuade pointed out that the Polo Grounds, situated in a "sparsely settled district, is practically soundproof so far as the surrounding residents of the neighborhood are concerned. It is my opinion that there is no infraction of any statute here. Playing baseball on the first day of the week, when not amounting to a serious interruption of the repose and religious liberty of the community, is not a violation of this section." (McQuade was also a rabid Giants fan who later became part-owner of the team.)

Even though the Giants avoided sanctions for the August 19 game, the team was reluctant to play any more Sunday games in the city until laws were passed that would clearly permit such an activity. (In 1918, along with Brooklyn and the Yankees, the Giants considered playing Sunday games at Harrison Field, a minor league stadium in Harrison, New Jersey, where Sunday baseball was allowed, but this never happened.)

The teams finally got the go-ahead for Sunday games in their own city when in April 1919 Governor Al Smith signed a state law that allowed local bodies to eliminate prohibitions of, among other things, baseball, fishing, and moving pictures on Sunday. Governor Smith declared that attending a Sunday baseball game is "in no sense deteriorating to the moral fiber," and added that

> well-to-do people can and do on Sunday pursue their amusements with entire impunity and under the protection of the laws. Our golf courses are crowded, our highways are thronged with automobiles seeking on Sunday a change of scene and the beneficial effects resulting therefrom. The activities of a poor man along this line are necessarily restricted by the limit of his means. It comes, however, within the reasonable reach of many to enjoy a baseball game and to obtain the rest which comes from recreation by such an outdoor health-giving amusement.

(Jimmy Walker, a future New York City mayor who was then a senator in the state assembly, was instrumental in getting the measure passed at the state level. According to Harold Seymour in *Baseball: The Golden Age*, Walker campaigned for mayor in 1925 under the slogan "Walker Gave Us Sunday Baseball.")

Given the approval of the state assembly, the New York City Board of Aldermen quickly passed an ordinance permitting Sunday baseball in the city, and the local teams altered their schedules to take advantage of the new law. The first Sunday of baseball in New York City was May 4, 1919, when a total of 60,000 fans showed up for either the Brooklyn-Boston game at Ebbets

Field in Brooklyn or for the New York-Philadelphia game at the Polo Grounds. Giants fans were disappointed with the result—the Phillies won the game, 4–3—but delighted with the continuing prospect of being able to watch baseball on Sunday.

Baseball provided a diversion for fans even though a day at the ballpark in the early part of the twentieth century didn't normally last as long as one in the latter part (unless, of course, a doubleheader was being played). The pace of games was much quicker for a lot of reasons, and there were times when a fan might spend more time on the commute to and from the Polo Grounds than actually at the stadium.

The extreme example of quick games came the day after the conclusion of the 1913 regular season. The Giants had won the National League pennant and were slated to start the World Series, against the Philadelphia Athletics, the next day. Rather than take a day off and rest, the Giants scheduled an exhibition game against the Philadelphia Phillies as a tuneup. Approximately 500 fans came to the Polo Grounds to see the game and the series of field events that preceded it. Hans Lobert of the Phillies won two of the events, a race around the bases and a 100-yard dash. The significant feature of the latter was that one of Lobert's vanquished opponents was New York outfielder Jim Thorpe, who had shined at the Stockholm Olympics the year before.

The game itself—won by the Giants, 4–1—moved nearly as fast as Lobert. "The chief aim of every player engaged in this was to hit the ball and see how far he could stretch his hit," reported the *New York Times* the next day. The players who hit safely often continued running until they were thrown out on the bases. In between innings, players raced to their positions as fast as they could, leaving little dead time. The entire game consumed 31 minutes, a professional record for a nine-inning game.

Of course, the 1913 Phillies-Giants contest was only an exhibition game. Five years later, however, the Giants were able to complete a full regular-season game at the Polo Grounds in under an hour. A scoreless game between the Giants and Brooklyn moved at an incredible pace; however, with neither team indicating a willingness to push a run across the plate, it appeared the contest might be headed for extra innings. But New York's Larry Doyle led off the last of the ninth with a single to right, moved to second on Artie Fletcher's bunt single, and continued on to third on a wild throw on the play. Heinie Zimmerman walked to load the bases. Bash Compton then ended the game with a single to left to bring in Doyle with the winning run. The game was completed in 56 minutes, a new major league record and one that lasted barely more than a year.

The record was broken at the Polo Grounds on the final day of the 1919 season in the first game of a doubleheader between the Giants and Phillies. Jess Barnes of the Giants won his twenty-fifth game of the year as New York beat Philadelphia, 6–1. According to the *New York Times:*

> There was no unusual effort yesterday to make a speed record until the Phils' half of the ninth. At that time it became apparent to the players that they could do something unusual, and for a half inning they hustled. Even with two out in the closing inning, [Fred] Luderus poked a hit to centre field, and he did not attempt to walk into any putout. Dave Bancroft did. He took a half swing at a ball, which rolled to Doyle, and the game was over. Bancroft's effort with two down in the ninth was the only part of the game in which real effort was lacking.

The game took only 51 minutes, a record for nine innings and only one minute longer than the major league record for a regular season game, set in a rain-shortened five-inning game by St. Louis and St. Paul of the Union Association in 1884.

A couple of other significant events in the early history of the rebuilt Polo Grounds were new ownership for the Giants and one last appearance by a famous fan. The fan was Frank B. Wood, famed for his shout of "Well! Well!" After an absence of seven years, Wood appeared at a game in 1914, reaching his seat as the Giants' "Turkey Mike" Donlin was taking his spot in the batter's box. Wood immediately let loose with his call—not with its usual splendor or volume but loud enough to be heard by Donlin, who stepped away from the plate long enough to tip his cap to Wood. Heywood Broun, reporting on Wood's death in December of that year, said not only had Wood's voice weakened but his optimism had dimmed as well. Wood had remained loyal to the Giants during a period around the turn of the century when their performance had reached its nadir. He kept his enthusiasm even when New York was behind by a sizable margin, and he once dressed down a fan who spoke derisively of the team after it had lost its twelfth straight game. "See here, young man," he scolded, "you can't expect this club to win all the time." In his 1914 appearance, however, Wood left the game with the Giants trailing by four runs in the seventh inning, never to be seen at the Polo Grounds again.

The change in ownership took place in 1919. John T. Brush had died in November of 1912, although the team remained in his family's hands until January 1919, when it was sold to a syndicate—operating under the name National Exhibition Company—headed by Charles A. Stoneham, John McGraw (also the manager of the team), and Frank McQuade (the New York magistrate who had dismissed the charges for the 1917 Sunday baseball game). Stoneham would end up as the last of the trio to have control of the team, and the Giants stayed in the Stoneham family (with son Horace taking over upon his father's death in 1935) through their remaining years in New York.

The first decade of the final version of the Polo Grounds closed on a sad note because of what happened in a game between the New York Yankees and Cleveland Indians on Monday, August 16, 1920. Neither team had yet won an American League pennant, but both were in the hunt for first place, along with the Chicago White Sox, as the Indians opened a series in New York. In the top of the fifth inning, Cleveland shortstop Ray Chapman stepped into the batter's box to face Carl Mays. Mays was a submarine pitcher—employing an underhand delivery—and his first pitch to Chapman was high and tight. The pitch ricocheted back toward Mays, who, thinking the ball had hit Chapman's bat, pounced on it and turned to throw to first. "But when I turned to throw to first base," Mays said the next day, "I had a horrible sensation that something was wrong." When Mays looked back toward home plate, he saw Chapman crumpled to the ground.

Although he had a fractured skull, Chapman was partially revived, and he attempted to walk across the field to the clubhouse. However, he collapsed again and had to be carried to the clubhouse and then taken to St. Lawrence Hospital near the Polo Grounds. At 4:40 the next morning, Chapman died. He remains the only player ever to die as a direct result of injuries suffered in a major league baseball game.

(Other deaths that may have been related to on-field injuries have occurred, however, most notably that of Mike "Doc" Powers, a catcher for the Philadelphia Athletics who died on April 26, 1909, following three operations for gangrenous poisoning of the intestines. The ailment began following the Athletics' season opener [and the first game ever played in Philadelphia's Shibe Park] on April 12, although the exact cause of the problem is unclear. One report says it was from internal injuries suffered when he crashed into a wall while chasing a pop fly in the game. Another maintains that he dislocated his intestine while straining upward to catch a pitch. The day after the season opener, Powers, who was a physician, said the illness that eventually took his life was acute indigestion caused by eating a cheese sandwich before the game. Although it can be debated whether Powers's death was caused by an injury in the game, there is no such dispute surrounding the circumstances of Ray Chapman's death.)

Budweiser
HUNTER WHISKEY
Hackett Carhart
CLOTHIERS
NO ERRORS
NATIONAL
CASH
REGISTERS
BROADWAY
PHILLIP MORRIS
Cigarettes
HATS

The Polo Grounds in 1908.

The 1909 New York Giants. Collection of Lawrence S. Ritter

Photographers and others gather at the site of the Polo Grounds after it had burned down in 1911. Library of Congress

A look at the new grandstand of the Polo Grounds, which was rebuilt after the 1911 fire. Note that the double-decked stands extend into fair territory in right field but are cut off in foul territory on the left-field side.

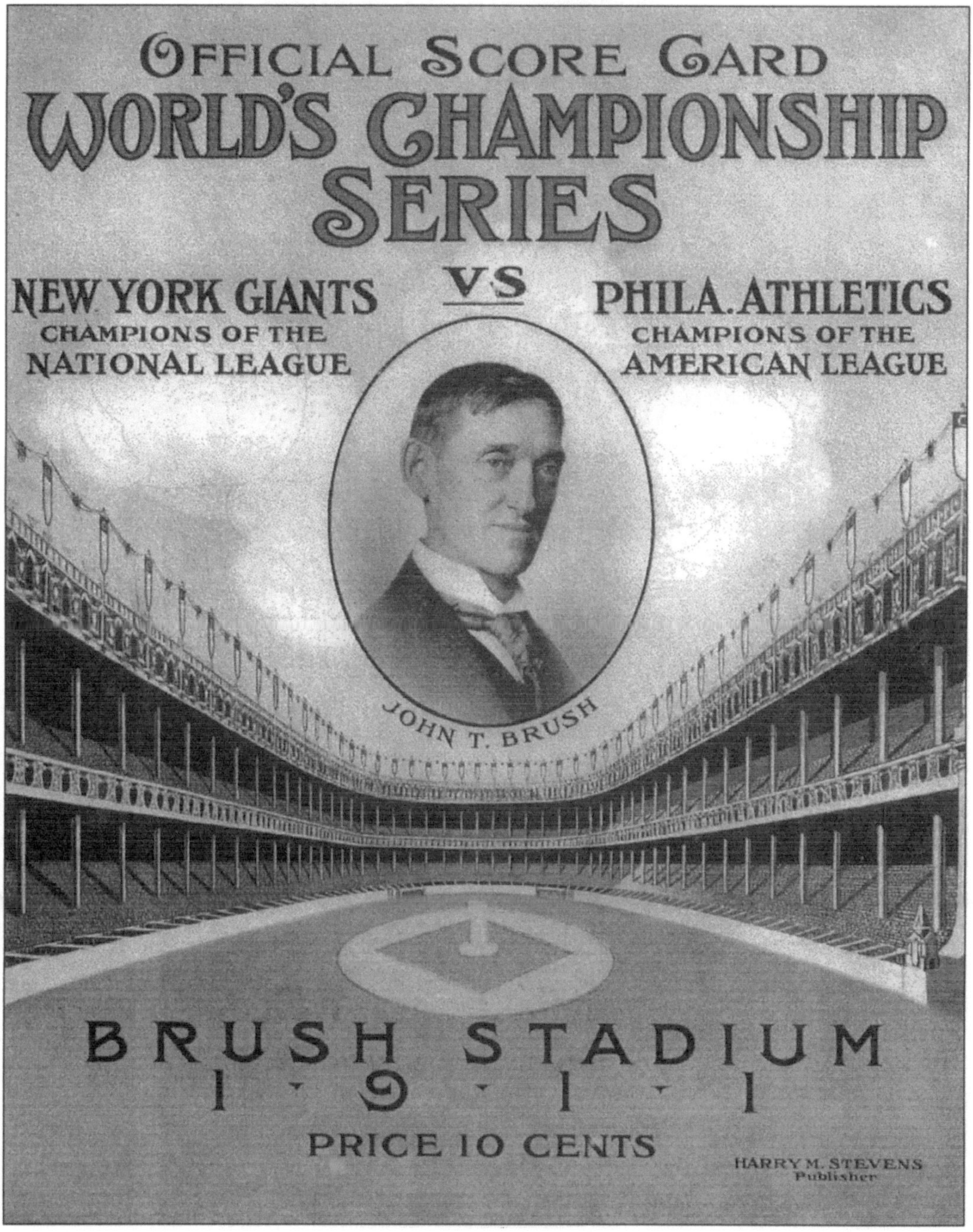

Owner John Brush was determined to have the new ballpark named after him and thus made sure the name Brush Stadium was on the cover of the program for the 1911 World Series. However, New Yorkers had different ideas, and the name Polo Grounds remained.

Scenes of the 1913 World Series at the Polo Grounds from a commemorative booklet issued by the Giants in 1914. Collection of Michael Frank

In 1923 the Yankees left the Polo Grounds for a home of their own across the Harlem River.

The extension of the grandstands, part of the construction that took place at the Polo Grounds after the 1922 season, created the overhang in left field, as shown here. Collection of Michael Frank

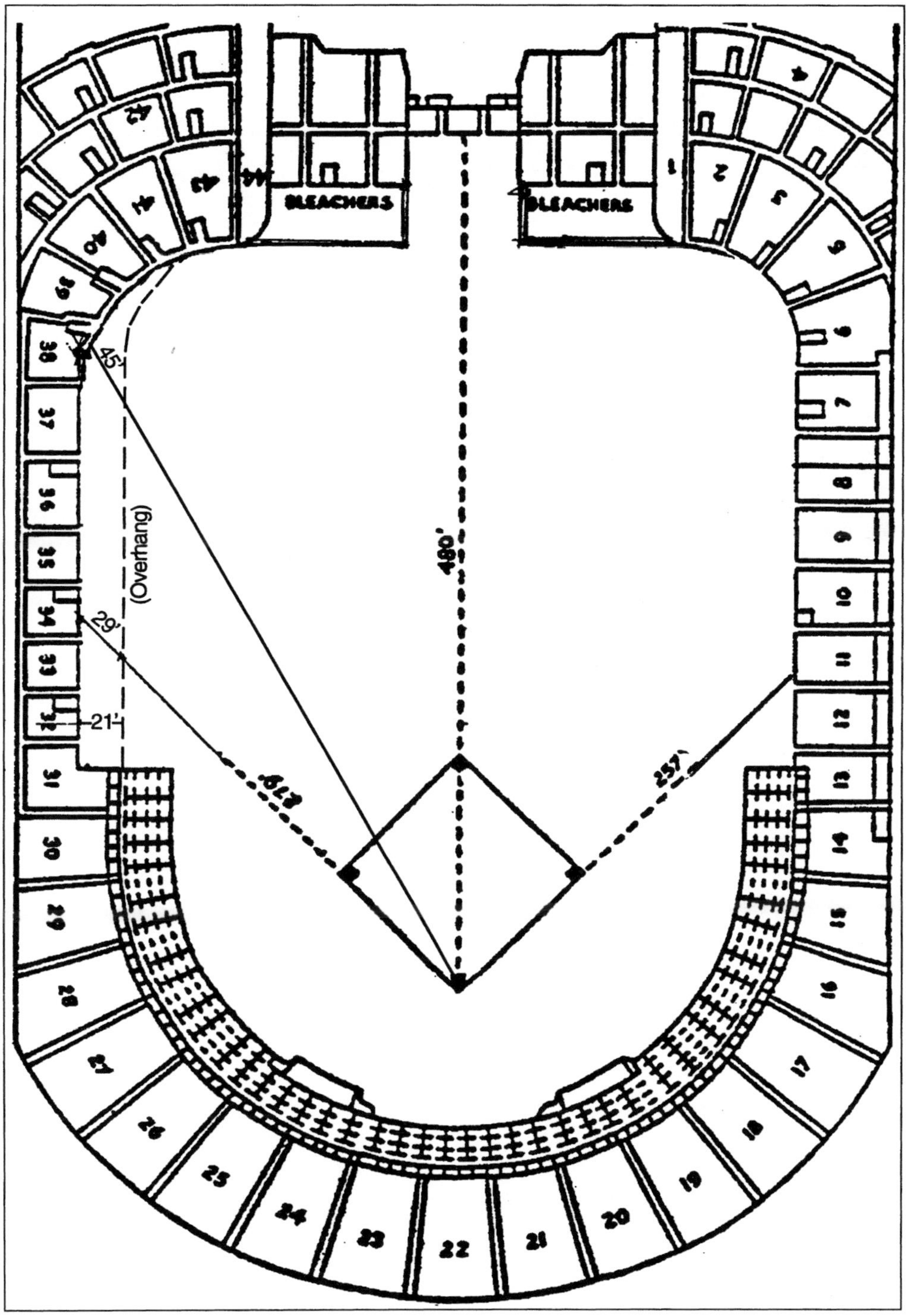

John Pastier, an architectural critic and stadium authority, has indicated the position of the overhang by plotting a dotted line on this diagram of the Polo Grounds. In addition to swallowing up high flies that wouldn't otherwise have reached the lower seats, the protrusion allowed some drives hit down the line to land in fair territory instead of curving foul before reaching the more distant lower grandstand.

The Polo Grounds with Yankee Stadium visible across the river, 1930s.

A view from right-center field at the 1934 season opener at the Polo Grounds. Transcendental Graphics

CHAPTER SEVEN

Home Runs and Hubbell

BASEBALL ENDURED A GREAT DEAL OF TRAUMA TOWARD THE END OF THE 1920 season. Six weeks after the death of Ray Chapman, eight members of the Chicago White Sox team that had won the American League pennant the previous year were indicted on charges of conspiring with gamblers to intentionally lose the 1919 World Series, an event that shook the integrity of the game and threatened its future.

Fortunately for baseball, there was excitement sufficient to overshadow the bad news, most of it the result of a player spending his first season with the Polo Grounds as his home field. As a member of the Boston Red Sox in 1919, Babe Ruth had set a major league record by hitting 29 home runs. The following season, Ruth surpassed his own mark with an incredible total of 54 homers. This time, he was doing it with the Polo Grounds as his home park, as he had been sold by the Red Sox to the New York Yankees following the 1919 season.

The left-handed-swinging Ruth definitely took a liking to his new digs in New York and took great advantage of the short distance down the line to right field in the Polo Grounds. With Fenway Park in Boston his home park in 1919, Ruth hit only 9 of his 29 home runs at home. In 1920, however, he hit 29 home runs at the Polo Grounds and only 25 on the road. If that doesn't seem like too great a discrepancy, consider that, for the season, Ruth had 50 more official at bats and 75 more plate appearances on the road than he had at home. No doubt, the Babe was ready to usher in the 1920s with an offensive performance never before seen in the game. Just as clear is the role the friendly dimensions of the Polo Grounds played in the barrage.

Back in the Polo Grounds in 1921, Ruth outdid himself again. For the third consecutive year, Ruth set a new major league single-season home run record, this time connecting 59 times (32 at the Polo Grounds and 27 on the road). Ruth's best-remembered season came several years later when he hit 60 home runs; however, his first two years in the Polo Grounds produced the two greatest overall offensive seasons ever in baseball.

In 1921, the Yankees finally won their first American League pennant (beginning a dynasty that would produce 29 pennants and 20 world championships over a span of 44 years). In the National League, the pennant winners were the New York Giants. Since both teams shared a stadium, it meant that the entire 1921 World Series was played in the Polo Grounds. The scene was repeated in 1922 as both the Yankees and Giants were again league champions.

Although the Yankees were making progress as a franchise, they were defeated by the Giants in both the 1921 and 1922 World Series. Even though the Giants were, in one sense, kings of the baseball world after winning two World Series in a row, in another sense, they weren't even kings of their own city, since they were being upstaged by their tenant, the Yankees, predominantly because of the exploits of Babe Ruth.

In 1920, the Babe's first year in Yankee pinstripes, the Yankees drew nearly 1.3 million fans to their games at the Polo Grounds (more than doubling their 1919 season attendance). The Yankees topped the million mark in attendance again in 1921 and 1922. The Giants had never drawn a million fans at home in one season (and wouldn't until 1945).

John McGraw was not the type of man to be magnanimous in such a situation. He was the type to be petty and vindictive. McGraw's jealousy of the Yankees' success is often cited as a reason for the Giants' decision to force the Yankees out of the Polo Grounds. However, there is much more to the story and a number of explanations of what transpired regarding the relations between the Yankees and Giants. In *Baseball: The Golden Age*, Harold Seymour wrote that the American League had been pressuring the Yankees to get their own stadium ever since 1915, when the team was acquired by Colonel Jacob Ruppert and Captain Tillinghast Huston. Another version, also noted in Seymour's book, has American League president Ban Johnson persuading the Giants to cancel the Yankees' lease as a means of ousting Ruppert and Huston as team owners.

What is clear is that in mid-May of 1920 (only a month into Ruth's first season with the Giants—hardly enough time for jealousy to set in), the

Giants informed the Yankees they would have to find a different place to play starting in 1921. Although it had been rumored for several years that the Giants might evict their tenants, the announcement caught the Yankees off guard. Ruppert said he had a reached verbal agreement in 1916 with the late John T. Brush's heirs—who operated the Giants at the time—that the Yankees would be welcome in the Polo Grounds for as long as they wanted to stay. But Giants' president Charles Stoneham, who had taken over the team from the Brush estate the previous year, said he was merely responding to the Yankees' statement that they would build their own stadium if they couldn't secure a long-term lease at the Polo Grounds. "We went over the matter carefully and replied that we believed it would be a good thing for baseball if they would build their own grounds, suggesting that they go right ahead with the enterprise," said Stoneham.

One week after the original announcement that the Yankees would have to find their own stadium, the Giants rescinded their eviction notice, but the Yankees had already begun efforts to find a new place to play. The team settled on a spot just across the Harlem River from the Polo Grounds, at 161st Street and River Avenue in the Bronx. The Yankees continued playing in the Polo Grounds until their new home, Yankee Stadium, was ready for the beginning of the 1923 season. Often called "The House That Ruth Built," Yankee Stadium—with its right-field fence within easy reach for a left-handed power hitter—was designed to take full advantage of its star occupant (although it still wasn't as friendly to the Babe as the Polo Grounds had been).

The end of the 1922 season marked not only the departure of the Yankees from the Polo Grounds but also a radical change in the look of the stadium. Initially the double-decked stands of Polo Grounds IV had resembled a hook more than a horseshoe. The stands reached approximately 40 feet into fair territory in right field but stopped short of the foul line in left field. Uncovered seats extended out from the permanent stands on both sides and eventually came together in center field.

Plans to renovate and enlarge the Polo Grounds started in 1921, when Charles Stoneham met with an architect to explore the possibility of increasing the seating capacity of the Polo Grounds from 38,000 to more than 50,000. In August of 1922 plans were filed with the Manhattan Bureau of Buildings for a massive project that would extend the double-decked grandstand on both the north (left-field) and south (right-field) sides of the stadium. The grandstands would then curve in toward one another but not actually come together. A uncovered bleacher section—itself divided by a building that housed the clubhouse and administrative offices—was to be wedged between the two grandstand sections in center field, with the clubhouse set back from the outfield fences along the bleachers, resulting in an alcove in straightaway center field. The area was in play, even the stairways on each side of the alcove that led to the Giants' and the visitors' clubhouses.

The massive clubhouse actually served as the center-field fence, although it was so far away that it didn't really matter. Stadium authority Phil Lowry has stated that he has never come across an example of a batted ball ever hitting the center-field clubhouse on the fly. He also indicated that it is unclear as to how high up on the clubhouse a drive would have had to have struck to be ruled an out-of-park home run. Lowry said it is possible that a drive hitting the clubhouse above a certain point, particularly where its wall sloped away from the field to create a beveled setback, may have counted as a home run. However, Lowry noted that the ground rules governing this are still a mystery, even after his interviews with many former players and umpires. Apparently no one gave the matter much thought, assuming—correctly—that it was a moot point.

Work on the stadium renovation began in November of 1922 with the removal of the old clubhouse. Construction proceeded through the winter and continued into the 1923 season. Fans attending the Giants' home opener in late April saw tall, red columns of steel in right and left field, towers for the pouring of concrete, and thousands of feet of timberwork, which were to become the concrete beds for thousands of new seats.

When construction was finally finished in mid-September of 1923, the Polo Grounds had assumed its final familiar look. "At the left-field foul pole, the concrete wall was 17 feet high, gradually rising to 18 feet in left center and then sloping to 12 feet where the left-field grandstand met the center-field bleachers," reported Lawrence S. Ritter in *Lost Ballparks.* "In right field, the wall was 11 feet high at the foul pole, gradually rising to 12 feet where the right-field grandstand met the center-field bleachers. The bleacher seats were behind 4-foot-high concrete walls topped by 4-foot-high wire screen."

So ample was the playing area that it was possible to fit the bullpens into fair territory with nary a chance that they would affect a ball in play. The visitors' bullpen was in left center and the home bullpen in right center, both approximately 440 feet from the plate. In addition, in the center-field alcove, just in front of the clubhouse, was a five-foot-high monument containing a tablet dedicated to Eddie Grant, a former Giant who was the first major league player killed in the World War. Dedicated on Decoration Day in 1921 (and remaining in deep center field after the stadium renovation), the plaque read:

IN MEMORY OF
CAPT. EDWARD LESLIE GRANT
307TH INFANTRY • 77TH DIVISION
A.E.F.
KILLED IN ACTION
ARGONNE FOREST
OCTOBER 5, 1918

PHILADELPHIA NATIONALS
1907 • 1908 • 1909 • 1910

CINCINNATI REDS
1911 • 1912 • 1913

NEW YORK GIANTS
1913 • 1914 • 1915

ERECTED BY FRIENDS IN BASEBALL,
JOURNALISM, AND THE SERVICE

Although the plaque remained, much else disappeared in the renovation, including a scoreboard in center. In the 1960s, the wall of the clubhouse would be used for a scoreboard, but for most of its existence the wall was either blank or the setting for huge advertisements. Also departing were the decorative friezes on the facade of the upper deck. Before the 1920s were out, the insignia of the National League teams had also been removed from the top of the grandstand.

One feature that did appear as a result of the extension of the grandstands was the overhang in left field. Until 1923, the double-decked grandstand on the left-field side had ended before it reached fair territory. With the extension, though, the upper deck extended over the playing field, 21 feet beyond the lower deck. (In right field, where the grandstand had already reached into fair territory before it was extended even farther, the upper and lower decks were flush. A photographers' perch that was later built on the front of the upper deck created a slight overhang—but nothing that approached the extreme of the overhang in left field.)

How often would the overhang turn otherwise catchable fly balls into home runs? John Pastier, an architect who grew up in New York and who has studied the geometry of baseball stadiums for nearly half a century, estimated that the bottom of the overhang was 35 feet above the ground. In terms of home runs, envision the trajectory a descending fly ball would need to clear a 35-foot-high barrier but not a 17-foot-high fence that was 21 feet farther away. (Consider also that, because of wind resistance and atmospheric drag, a fly ball would come down at a steeper trajectory than it went up.)

Pastier also pointed out that the effective distance of the overhang was actually greater than 21 feet. Figuring in the 135-degree angle of the foul line crossing the plane of the overhang and then meeting the fence of the lower grandstand, the distance between the overhang and the lower fence, as measured along the foul line, was actually 29 feet.

If the overhang wasn't the cause of enough frustration for outfielders, it made fly catching difficult even when the ball didn't settle in the upper deck. Fred Stein, author of *Under Coogan's Bluff,* said the overhang meant "that in cases where fly balls just missed the upper deck there was a split second during which the fielder frequently lost sight of the ball."

While the look of the Polo Grounds received its last radical change with the 1922–23 expansion, most aspects of the baseball experience beneath Coogan's Bluff remained constant, including the setting. Behind the stadium rose the first portion of the bluff itself, which leveled out briefly for the Harlem River Speedway. A road that still exists (although it is now Harlem River Drive), the Speedway has an interesting history of its own. When it opened in 1898 (with 155th Street as the southern terminus), it was used primarily by harness enthusiasts for trotting-horse trials. It was made a parkway in 1915 and eventually extended southward to hook up with the East River (now Franklin D. Roosevelt) Drive. Although many fans entered the Polo Grounds on the Eighth Avenue side, others came to the stadium along the Speedway. For them, ramps sloped down to a series of small buildings where tickets could be purchased. A different set of ramps took patrons down even farther to the upper and lower seating levels.

From the Speedway, the rocky crag continued upward to Edgecombe Avenue, where the land again leveled out to the west. On this high ground, between Edgecombe Avenue and Jumel Place, was the Jumel Mansion (now the Morris-Jumel Mansion), a 1765 structure that served as British and American army headquarters during the Revolutionary War. Converted in 1903 into a period museum (a function it still holds), the mansion offers a commanding view of the area, which included the Polo Grounds and a portion of its playing field. While the Washington Headquarters Association, operators of the museum, discouraged fans from loitering on the grounds to watch a game, there were many other vantage points in this general vicinity, along the top of Coogan's Bluff, that offered glimpses of the action.

And even though that was usually all that was available—a glimpse—the bluff was a popular spot, particularly during World Series. Milton Bracker, who later covered the Giants as a newspaper reporter, recalled the experience in Joseph Durso's book *The Days of Mr. McGraw*. Bracker said that although the pitcher, catcher, first baseman, and right fielder were rarely visible, "you always got to see the shortstop, the left fielder, and the center fielder. You saw the second baseman on plays near the base and the third baseman on plays away from it. . . . The combination of the scoreboard [in center field that was removed after the 1922 season], a clear view of second base, and an average of four players was just like being at the game."

Bracker was present on the bluff for the final game of the 1921 World Series, which ended on an unusual play. The Yankees had Aaron Ward on first when Frank "Home Run" Baker hit a hard grounder toward right that Giants second baseman Johnny Rawlings dived for and snagged. Rawlings threw to first baseman George Kelly to retire Baker. Kelly then fired across the diamond to Frankie Frisch to nail Ward trying to advance to third, finishing the game and giving the Giants the world championship. Here is Bracker's description:

> Those on the bluff couldn't see any of these players but they knew exactly what was at stake. . . . Baker ripped one to the right side. From the bluff, the second baseman, Johnny Rawlings, was seen to dive to his own left and disappear from view. An incredulous roar welled up from the stands. Ward, sure the ball had gone through, rounded second and headed for third. (Right in front of every man and boy on the bluff!) Then he dived, too, for a long slide around third that found Frankie Frisch waiting for him with the game's final tag. It was the famous Rawlings-to-Kelly-to-Frisch double play that gave the Giants the series and gave everyone who saw it one of the big thrills of his baseball life.

In 1923, the Giants and Yankees met in the World Series for the third straight year. There were two differences in the 1923 series, however. First, the Polo Grounds was not the site for all the games, since the Yankees now had their own stadium. The other change was the victor. The Yankees, after having been defeated in the World Series by the Giants the previous two years, this time won the series, four games to two.

Having their own stadium didn't necessarily help the Yankees in the series; the Giants' only two wins came in Yankee Stadium, and both were the result of home runs by their aging, but still colorful, outfielder Casey Stengel.

(The first game, at Yankee Stadium, was won by the Giants as Stengel broke a 4–4 tie with an inside-the-park home run to left center in the ninth inning. In Game 3, at Yankee Stadium, the Giants won, 1–0, on a seventh-inning homer by Stengel into the right-field stands.) However, the Yankees won the other game in their home park and took all three games in the Polo Grounds to capture their first world championship.

The Yankees' string of league championships was broken in 1924 but not the Giants', who won their fourth consecutive National League pennant (giving them 10 since the turn of the century and 12 overall). The Giants were, however, defeated in the World Series by the Washington Senators in 1924. This also marked the Giants' last appearance in the World Series under John McGraw, who managed for another seven-and-a-half years but had no more pennant winners.

During this period and in ensuing years, McGraw and others were honored with plaques that were added to the lower portion of the clubhouse wall in center field (with Eddie Grant's memorial already on a freestanding monument in front of the clubhouse). Between games of a doubleheader between the Giants and Cubs in September of 1928, two plaques were unveiled for former Giants stars. One was for Christy Mathewson, the great pitcher who had died of tuberculosis in 1925, the other for outfielder Ross Youngs, who had died of Bright's disease at the age of 30 in October of 1927. Mathewson and Youngs were said to have been the favorite players of John McGraw, who died in February 1934 and had a plaque placed in his honor on the clubhouse wall in ceremonies preceding that summer's All Star Game at the Polo Grounds.

McGraw had retired in June of 1932 and was succeeded as manager by Bill Terry, who was also the team's first baseman. An outstanding hitter, Terry had produced a batting average of .401 in 1930. He was still potent with the bat and continued to use it, assuming the duties of player-manager. In Terry's first full season, 1933, the Giants won their first pennant in nine years and returned to the World Series, again facing the Washington Senators (their opponent in their last World Series, in 1924). This time the Giants prevailed, beating the Senators, four games to one.

Terry's managerial career may best be remembered for a snide remark he made prior to the 1934 season that came back to haunt him. When asked by a reporter about the Brooklyn Dodgers, Terry replied, "Is Brooklyn still in the league?" The Dodgers kept that slight in mind all year and got special pleasure out of defeating New York twice on the final weekend of the season, depriving the Giants of a chance at another pennant as the St. Louis Cardinals pulled past them to win the National League championship. The Giants did win two more pennants during Terry's reign as manager—which lasted through the 1941 season—but were defeated in the World Series by the New York Yankees in both 1936 and 1937.

At the time, Carl Hubbell was not only the Giants' top pitcher but also one of the best in baseball. "The Meal Ticket," as he was known because of his value to the Giants, "King Carl" was a southpaw with a devastating screwball. (A screwball is a curve ball that breaks in the opposite direction. It had also been Christy Mathewson's best pitch, although it had then been known as a fadeaway.)

Hubbell was the starting pitcher for the National League in the 1934 All Star Game, played at the Polo Grounds, and faced a starting lineup of American League players who are all now in the Baseball Hall of Fame. When the first two batters—Charlie Gehringer of Detroit and Heinie Manush of Washington—reached base, Hubbell was in a jam. But he got out of it by striking out Babe Ruth, Lou Gehrig, and Jimmie Foxx. He continued with the strikeouts in the second inning, fanning Al Simmons and Joe Cronin before giving up a single to Bill Dickey. Hubbell then closed out the inning by striking out Lefty Gomez, the American League starting pitcher. Striking out six future Hall of Famers, including five in a row, was one of the highlights of Hubbell's career, which also included a streak of 24 consecutive victories over the 1936 and 1937 seasons.

While Hubbell was the New York ace on the mound, the batting parade was led by a powerful left-handed hitter who was well suited for the strange dimensions of the Polo Grounds. Mel Ott had joined the Giants as a 17-year-old and became one of the best sluggers in baseball. He had a distinctive batting style, leaning back and lifting his front leg as the pitch was delivered, then bringing the leg down as he swung the bat—often with devastating results.

Many players have taken advantage of the peculiarities of their home stadium but perhaps none as successfully as Ott. Of his 511 career home runs (a National League record at the time of his retirement), 323 were hit at the Polo Grounds and only 188 on the road. While this might lead some to diminish Ott's achievements, Giants' historian Fred Stein points out that there is more to the story. "Closer examination shows that the Polo Grounds' advantage was significant only in the latter part of his [Ott's] career, 1939–47, when his power had waned," wrote Stein in his 1991 article "No Cheap Homers for Ott." "In those years 75 percent of his homers were hit at home. However, during Ott's prime hitting years, 1928–38, only 58 percent were hit at the

Polo Grounds." Stein also noted that although the Polo Grounds bolstered Ott's home run totals, the ballpark did not necessarily contribute to his overall batting record:

> Over his first nine seasons as a regular, Ott's [batting] average was .343 on the road and .286 at home. Over his career, he batted 14 points higher on the road than at home and hit significantly more singles, doubles, and triples away from home. In 1929, he set still-existing National League road records for runs (79) and runs batted in (87). This would indicate that in parks where his pull-hitting ability might be wasted, he often went with the pitch rather than pulling the ball. In other words, about 130 doubles on the road were turned into home runs at the Polo Grounds.
>
> Ott was a Hall of Fame hitter wherever he played, but he was especially deadly at his home field, the Polo Grounds.

As for the home runs Ott hit at the Polo Grounds, Stein claimed they were "typically not rainbow-shaped bloop hits in the 260–280-foot range but well-stroked drives into the upper stands."

One of Ott's greatest fans was actress Tallulah Bankhead, described by Stein as "perhaps the most baseball-happy stage figure of the time." Bankhead helped carry on the tradition, started in the 1880s, of the Giants being the baseball favorites of entertainers and Broadway personalities. Her favorite Giant was Mel Ott, whom she could readily identify by the number 4 on the back of his uniform. Although she denied the story, Bankhead was reported once to have ventured to a game at Ebbets Field in Brooklyn, where she spent the afternoon rooting for Dolf Camilli (who wore number 4 for the Dodgers), thinking he was Ott. She also attended the 1939 All Star Game, played at Yankee Stadium, and was said to be in a state of confusion as there appeared to be four different Mel Otts playing for the National League squad (which, in addition to Ott and Camilli, had two other players with the number 4: Billy Herman of the Chicago Cubs and Ernie Lombardi of the Cincinnati Reds).

Mel Ott succeeded Bill Terry as manager of the Giants in 1942 and, as Terry had, continued as an active player for several seasons. His tenure as manager was not nearly as successful as his playing career, however. The Giants twice finished in last place under Ott, who was replaced as manager by Leo Durocher during the 1948 season.

Ott had retired as an active player the previous September, although his 1947 season had consisted of only four pinch-hitting appearances, in which he went hitless. Even though he contributed nothing offensively in 1947, the Giants set a new major league record by hitting 221 home runs. Johnny Mize led the way with 51 (a total that tied him with Ralph Kiner of Pittsburgh for the league lead), while Willard Marshall hit 36, Walker Cooper hit 35, and

Bobby Thomson hit 29. Even with these enormous home run totals, the Giants finished in fourth place.

Despite the mediocre finish of the team, the exploits of the power hitters generated enough excitement for the Giants to draw more than 1.6 million fans to the Polo Grounds in 1947, the team's all-time high during their years in New York. Only two years before, in 1945, the Giants had broken the million mark in attendance for the first time, a notable achievement considering that World War II was still being fought during most of the season. Many of the game's best players—and fans—were still in the service overseas. In the ensuing years, the Giants—like other major league teams—reveled in the postwar prosperity and drew more than a million fans a season seven more times over the next nine years.

One factor in the increasing attendance was the arrival of night baseball. The Giants had been one of the teams that fought the idea of night games when it was first introduced in the major leagues at Crosley Field in Cincinnati in 1935. Not only did the team decide not to install a lighting system at the Polo Grounds, but manager Bill Terry made it clear that other teams in the league should not schedule night games when the Giants were visiting.

At the end of the 1939 season, however, the Giants' management made the decision to install lights at the Polo Grounds, even though Terry remained as vociferous as ever in his opposition. The Polo Grounds already had some low-altitude lights to help illuminate the field during football games, but nothing of the magnitude needed to make it bright enough to play baseball after the sun had gone down. That changed in 1940, as the steelwork for the light standards began in January. The towers were up within two months, and the lights in place by the first of April. Eight steel towers, each weighing 160 tons and extending 150 feet above the field, were supported by steel platforms on the grandstand roof and connected to grandstand columns. With 836 high-powered bulbs, the lighting system was the most powerful of any in the world at the time.

Although the Giants now had the capability, they moved slowly into night baseball. Only seven night games were scheduled for the Polo Grounds in 1940, the first coming on Friday, May 24, in a game against the Boston Bees, managed by Casey Stengel. (From 1936 to 1940, the Boston Braves—now the Atlanta Braves—were known as the Bees.) Mayor Fiorello La Guardia threw out the first ball at the game, which the Giants won, 8–1, before a crowd of more than 22,000. For the first time, New York also agreed to play some night games on the road that season.

As time went on, and the advent of night baseball proved popular, the Giants and other teams scheduled more and more games for the evening. The Polo Grounds even hosted the first All Star Game at night, in 1942. The game was scheduled to begin at 6:30 P.M., qualifying it as a night game, although it started even later after a rain delay of nearly an hour. (That year's All Star Game had originally been scheduled for Ebbets Field in Brooklyn. However, since the proceeds from the game were slated for war charities and the Polo Grounds could accommodate more fans, the Dodgers allowed the site to be switched. Unfortunately, the rain kept many fans away, and the attendance was 34,178, far below the stadium's capacity.) In the game, home runs accounted for all the scoring, as the American League beat the National League, 3–1.

Lou Boudreau of Cleveland led off the game with a home run to left, and Detroit's Rudy York later tucked a two-run homer around the right-field foul pole. Brooklyn's Mickey Owen homered for the National League's only run—even though he would not hit a home run during the entire season. However, according to baseball historian David Pietrusza, the outcome of the game was not the evening's main story. A citywide blackout drill was scheduled for 9:30 that night, and the last out of the game was made with barely two minutes to spare. "As the contest ended," Pietrusza said, "everything went dark—streets, stands, elevated stations, locker rooms, everything. Both teams lingered in darkened clubhouses for 20 minutes before lights returned. Thirty-five thousand fans tarried in their seats, amusing themselves with a community-sing while they waited to leave the park."

An unusual game was played at the Polo Grounds on Monday night, June 26, 1944—a three-sided round-robin contest involving the Giants, Yankees, and Dodgers. The exhibition—which drew more than 50,000 fans, with the proceeds used for war bonds—featured an array of pregame festivities, including Milton Berle presiding over a musical show and the introduction of many former New York baseball greats. The game itself consisted of each of the teams taking a turn sitting out for a full inning while the other two played that inning in the field and at bat. The sequence continued for a full nine innings, with each of the teams having the chance to play six complete innings. The final score was Dodgers 5, Yankees 1, Giants 0. Here is the line score from that contest:

Inning	**1**	**2**	**3**	**4**	**5**	**6**	**7**	**8**	**9**
Dodgers	1	2	X	0	0	X	0	2	X —5
Yankees	0	X	0	0	X	0	0	X	1 —1
Giants	X	0	0	X	0	0	X	0	0 —0

During this period, the look of the Polo Grounds continued to change—not as dramatically as in the 1920s, when the grandstands were extended, but in ways that were noticeable. By the mid-1940s, a pair of batter's eyes—backdrops to help batters see the pitches more clearly—had been placed atop the bleacher walls on either side of the alcove in center field. Each measuring 20 feet wide and 17 feet high, "they guarded each side of the runway leading to the clubhouse like the impassive lions in front of the main building of the New York Public Library on Fifth Avenue," according to Ritter in *Lost Ballparks.*

Advertisements on the outfield walls disappeared before the 1948 season. Gone were the colorful signs for products like Coca-Cola, Gem Razors, Burma-Shave, and Botany Ties. The reason was that the Chesterfield cigarette company, which had erected a large ad on the massive clubhouse wall in center field, didn't want the competition from other advertisers, even those with noncompeting products. In return for paying $250,000 for the broadcast rights to Giants games on radio and television in 1948, Chesterfield demanded that all other advertising on outfield walls be taken down. "After that, the walls were painted a restful green to conform with the rest of the park, which may not have pleased the outfielders who had used the letters in the advertisements as reference points in judging rebounds," wrote Fred Stein in *Under Coogan's Bluff.*

In the 1960s, the clubhouse wall in center was finally used for a scoreboard, but until that time, hand-operated scoreboards were squeezed on to the facing of the upper deck near the foul poles in left and right field.

During the 1940s, the lineup of plaques on the center-field clubhouse wall had a few additions. On Sunday, December 2, 1945, plaques were added to honor two former members of the New York Giants football team (which used the Polo Grounds as its home from 1925 to 1955) who had been killed in World War II. One was for Jack Lummus, an end with the Giants in 1941 who had joined the Marines Corps in early 1942. As a platoon leader of the Second Battalion, Twenty-Seventh Marines, Fifth Marine Division, Lummus was awarded the Congressional Medal of Honor for actions on Iwo Jima in 1945, when he had both legs blown off by a Japanese land mine. "Looks like the Giants have lost a damn good end," he remarked before dying of his wounds. The other plaque was for Al Blozis, a tackle for the Giants from 1942 through 1945. In January of 1945 (just a few weeks after he had played in the National Football League title game between the Giants and Green Bay Packers), Blozis, a lieutenant, was in combat in France. He ventured into a snowstorm in search of one of his men and was never seen again.

In July of 1948, another plaque was unveiled to honor Jimmy Walker, the former New York mayor who had died 18 months before. Although Walker had been forced to resign his office amid a scandal in 1932, he was remembered fondly by area baseball fans for his earlier efforts to legalize Sunday baseball in the city. His Polo Grounds plaque read, "Friend and Fan, whose Sunday baseball law made it possible for millions of his fellow citizens to enjoy the game."

Even the area outside the Polo Grounds was changing during this time. In the late 1940s, the repair yards for the subway and elevated trains were demolished and replaced by the Colonial Park housing project.

Inside the stadium, changes in policy were made in the late 1940s to help the players get to the clubhouse after games without having to interact with the fans on the field. It was the end of a quaint tradition and one that usually posed no problems for either the players or the fans. Stan Isaacs, who later covered the Giants as a reporter, recalled his first game at the Polo Grounds in the 1930s, when he walked with his dad across the field toward the exit in center field and saw Rip Collins of the Cubs next to them. Issacs's dad suggested that he ask for an autograph. Young Stan replied, "No, he's not a Giant."

Player-fan relations weren't always that cordial, however. Following a Dodger-Giant game in April 1949, a Brooklyn fan claimed that he was punched and kicked by New York manager Leo Durocher. Commissioner A. B. "Happy" Chandler finally cleared Durocher of the charges, but the Giants management took action to prevent such encounters in the future. Fans could still exit by their usual route, but they would have to wait until the players and umpires had reached their dressing rooms before going onto the field. After the first night in which the policy was in effect, the *New York Sun* reported, "It was a strange sight, for the Polo Grounds at least, to see players of both teams walking leisurely the length of the field to the clubhouse, rather than making the customary mad dash and being forced to sidestep the usual number of autograph hunters and cap snatchers."

Allowing fans to amble across the field didn't make it any easier to maintain the field, not that these were easy grounds to maintain in the first place. Work had to be done on the field every fall and winter to offset the natural falling away that occurred due to the quicksand that underlay it. The tendency of the Polo Grounds to sink was increased by the subway line that ran beneath the adjacent parking lot. In the mid-1940s, the Giants spent more than $125,000 to raise the field—using approximately 3,000 cubic yards of gravel, 1,500 cubic yards of top soil, and 160,000 square feet of sod—and improve the drainage. This helped with some of the problems, but the job was still a challenging one for the groundskeeper.

Fortunately, by this time the Giants had one of the best, Matty Schwab. Schwab was always close at hand to take care of any problem—very close, since his home was beneath the left-field stands. For seven years, he had been the superintendent for Ebbets Field in Brooklyn, where he was responsible for the entire facility, not just the playing area, even though the latter was all he was really interested in. A third-generation groundskeeper (Schwab's grandfather and father had both tended ballparks in Cincinnati), Schwab was amenable to Horace Stoneham's offer to come to the Giants in 1946 and be in charge of nothing more than the field.

His first year with the Giants, Schwab and his family—wife Rose and son Jerry—moved into the Concourse Plaza Hotel near Yankee Stadium in the Bronx, but the living arrangements were far from ideal. Schwab tinkered with the idea of moving back to Brooklyn but hated the thought of the long commute to and from the Polo Grounds. Instead, he talked Stoneham into converting some empty space under the left-field stands into an apartment. A roll-up door on the left-field fence, just to the left of the foul pole, led under the stands to the entrance of the apartment, which consisted of a kitchen, bathroom, living room, and a bedroom that was used by Jerry. The apartment did have windows, but none offered much of a view. All that could be seen was the concourse between the apartment and the area outside the ballpark to the north (which first consisted of the repair yards for the subway and elevated cars and then high-rise housing). It was possible for the family to exit the stadium through another roll-up door on the outside stadium wall, although normally they went via car, driving through the concourse under the stands in back of home plate and continuing around the entire stadium until they emerged through a door on Eighth Avenue, underneath the grandstand in right-center field.

Being on site at all times was handy for Schwab, who—helped by his son—often got up every few hours at night to move the large sprinklers around the field. Sometimes Jerry would camp overnight in the outfield with his friends, who included Leo Durocher's son Chris; Dale Jansen, son of Giants pitcher Larry Jansen; and the sons of clubhouse manager Eddie Logan, Roger and Ed, Jr. "Jerry Schwab was my best friend, and I often stayed with him and his folks, Matty and Rose, under those stands," recalled Ed Logan, Jr. "We had a Little League team of Jerry, sons of various players, and me. Matty let us use the field when the Giants were out of town. We used to hit golf balls from home plate and ride our bikes up and down the stands during the away dates also."

Jerry and Rose Schwab returned to the family's regular home in Florida in September, at the start of the school year, but Matty wasn't able to join them until December, after both the baseball and football seasons had ended. At least he would have the small apartment to himself for a few months in the fall and again in the spring—before the school year ended and the rest of the family came north to join him.

For many of the seasons between 1935 and 1950, the Polo Grounds served as a home to another baseball team besides the Giants—the New York Cubans of the Negro National League (or Negro American League after 1948, when the Negro National League Disbanded). The Cubans were owned by Alex Pompez, a sports promoter with a seamier sideline. "Capitalizing on his baseball contacts and reputation, Pompez entered the numbers business in the twenties and became an important cog in the Dutch Schultz mob and a prime figure in the Harlem rackets," wrote Donn Rogosin in his book on the Negro Leagues, *Invisible Men.* "Due to Harlem's preeminent position in black life, Pompez was among the most illustrious black-community gangsters in the nation by the mid thirties."

Through the years the Cubans had a number of outstanding players, including infielders Minnie Minoso, Dick Lundy, George Crowe, Ray Dandridge (now a member of the baseball Hall of Fame), and Lyman Bostock, Sr., and pitchers Luis Tiant, Sr. (who had a win-loss record of 10–0 with three shutouts in the Cubans' pennant-winning season of 1947), Chet Brewer, Dave Barnhill, and Martin Dihigo (another Hall of Famer who could and did play all positions on the diamond).

The Polo Grounds hosted two Negro World Series games. One was the opener of the 1946 series between the Newark Eagles of the Negro National League and the Kansas City Monarchs of the Negro American League. Newark was led by pitcher Leon Day and hitters like Larry Doby (who had led the National League in batting average), Monte Irvin, Johnny Davis, and Lenny Pearson. The Monarchs, on the other hand, had stars like John "Buck" O'Neil, Hank Thompson, Connie Johnson, and Satchel Paige, one of the greatest pitchers ever—in any league.

Paige didn't start the game but entered as a reliever for Hilton Smith in the sixth inning and gave up a single to Davis that brought in a run to tie the game, 1–1. In the top of the seventh, Paige led off with a single and later scored what proved to be the winning run. The crowd of 19,435 was nearly double the attendance of that afternoon's game between the Giants and St. Louis Cardinals at the Polo Grounds.

In 1947, the New York Cubans made it to the Negro World Series, facing the Cleveland Buckeyes of the Negro American League. Only the first game of the series was at the Polo Grounds, and rain interrupted the contest three times. The game never resumed after the final delay, in the seventh inning. Cleveland had scored a run to take the lead, 6–5, in the top of the seventh. However, since the game was rained out before the Cubans' half of the inning was completed, the run was nullified, and the game ended as a 5–5 tie. The Cubans eventually won the series, four games to one, with the ensuing games being played at Yankee Stadium, Comiskey Park in Chicago, Shibe Park in Philadelphia, and League Park in Cleveland.

Although no more Negro World Series were played at the Polo Grounds, there were more memorable moments involving the Negro Leagues, including a game in 1948 when Luke Easter of the Homestead Grays became the first player to homer into the center-field bleachers since the stadium had been remodeled the early 1920s.

In 1949 the New York Cubans became an official farm team of the New York Giants, the only Negro League team to serve such a function for a major league team in organized baseball. As a farm team, the Cubans were to provide players to the Giants and their minor league system. In June of 1949, Dave Barnhill and Ray Dandridge moved from the Cubans to the Minneapolis Millers, the Giants' top minor league team. That was as far as they got, however. Neither one ever reached the major leagues, nor did many other great stars from the New York Cubans and other Negro League teams.

The first blacks to play for the Giants, Monte Irvin and Hank Thompson, did not even enter the Giants farm system from the New York Cubans. Monte Irvin was signed away from the Newark Eagles, and Thompson—who had briefly played in the major leagues with the St. Louis Browns of the American League in 1947—was a member of the Kansas City Monarchs prior to joining the Giants organization in 1949 and being assigned to a farm team in Jersey City. Both Thompson and Irvin made their Giants debuts on Friday, July 8—Thompson starting the game at second base and Irvin entering as a pinch hitter in the eighth inning.

Integration of organized baseball was underway—but not at a rapid pace. Still, the Giants moved more quickly than most teams in opening their ranks to dark-skinned players. Beyond being a socially conscious move, dropping the barriers provided a means of tapping tremendous baseball talent. It didn't take long for the Giants to realize the benefits of this, as working his way toward the major leagues was a young black man who would become one of the most exciting players in the history of the Polo Grounds.

CHAPTER EIGHT

The Final Years

IN THE LATE 1940S, WILLIE MAYS HIT HIS FIRST HOME RUN IN THE POLO Grounds—for the Birmingham Black Barons in a game against the New York Cubans.

By June of 1950, Mays was in the Giants organization and working his way back to the Polo Grounds. He spent the rest of the season with the Trenton Giants in the Interstate League before progressing to the Minneapolis Millers of the American Association in 1951 but didn't stay long before making the final jump to the major leagues. After 35 games with the Millers, Mays had a batting average of .477 and was leading the league in a number of other offensive categories while performing brilliantly in center field. He was too good to keep in the minors any longer, and on May 24 he received the call to join the Giants.

New York was playing a weekend series in Philadelphia when Mays made his debut, which wasn't a memorable one. He was hitless in five at bats against the Phillies and drew the collar again in the next two games.

But then the Giants came home. Mays made his first Polo Grounds appearance as a member of the New York Giants, and this time it *was* memorable. Facing Warren Spahn of the Boston Braves in the last of the first inning, Mays connected for a towering fly ball that landed on top of the left-field roof, the first of 660 home runs Mays would hit in the major leagues. Mays played well enough to be named the National League Rookie of the Year in 1951, but the season will be remembered better because of the tremendous pennant race, possibly the best since 1908. As before, the Polo Grounds was a focal point in the battle.

For much of the season, it didn't look like there would be any race in the National League. On August 11, the Brooklyn Dodgers held a 13½ game lead over the Giants. But from there, New York went on a 16-game winning streak and closed out its schedule with 37 wins in 44 games. When the regular season ended, both the Giants and Dodgers had records of 96 wins and 58 losses. A three-game playoff was necessary to determine the 1951 league champion.

The Giants and Dodgers split the first two games; the decisive third game was at the Polo Grounds on Wednesday, October 3. Brooklyn carried a 4–1 lead into the last of the ninth inning, but the Giants rallied. Alvin Dark and Don Mueller singled. After Monte Irvin fouled out, Whitey Lockman doubled to left, bringing home Dark and sending Mueller sliding into third. Mueller was safe on the play, although he severely injured his ankle. The tension mounted during the delay as Mueller was carried off the field. Clint Hartung came in to run for him while the Dodgers changed pitchers, Ralph Branca relieving starter Don Newcombe.

Finally, play resumed. Branca's first pitch to Bobby Thomson was a strike. Thomson turned on the next pitch and lifted a fly toward left. In many, if not all, of the other stadiums in the major leagues, it likely would have been nothing more than a fly out. But this was the Polo Grounds. As Brooklyn left fielder Andy Pafko stood at the fence, the 315-foot marker near his feet, he stared up helplessly as the fly settled into the lower grandstand, a three-run homer to give the Giants the game, 5–4, and the National League championship.

In the broadcast booths, while Ernie Harwell described the play for television viewers, on the radio side Russ Hodges was shouting into the microphone his rendition that would become a classic in the annals of sports announcing: "The Giants win the pennant . . . . The Giants win the pennant."

Although the Giants couldn't carry the momentum into the World Series—they lost, four games to two, to the Yankees—Thomson's "Shot Heard 'Round the World" remains one of the most famous ever hit and has often been cited as the most memorable moment in baseball history. Baseball historian John McCormack—who attended many games at the Polo Grounds between 1924 and 1953, including the 1951 playoff finale—disputed the claim that Thomson's drive was nothing more than a "Polo Grounds home run." After a writer said Thomson's homer "looped into the shorter lower left field stands," McCormack responded:

> Neither Bobby Thomson nor anyone else "looped" a homer into the lower left field stands at the Polo Grounds. Thomson hit a line drive, the only type drive that could get into those stands. There were a lot of cheap home runs hit at the Polo Grounds. But none went into the lower left field stands. Why? Because of the Polo Grounds' curious configuration. The upper left field stands jutted out over the lower stands perhaps 15 to 20 feet. As a result, any looping drive that didn't get into the upper stands would hit the façade for a home run or be caught by the left fielder. There was no way it could fall into the lower left field stands. . . . Thomson's drive would have been a home run at Ebbets Field or most of the National League parks of the time. It was no cheap drive.

John Pastier, the expert on stadium geometry, said the distance on the home run could have been as short as 340 feet (the spot of the field-level landing point had there been no obstructions) and as much as 355 feet, although he stated the latter figure is "stretching it." Had the distance been 350 feet, Pastier claimed, it would have been an out in most other ballparks:

> That [the 350-foot distance] would make it catchable in Ebbets Field [Brooklyn], Shibe Park [Philadelphia], Sportsman's Park [St. Louis], Forbes Field [Pittsburgh], Wrigley Field [Chicago], and most likely even Crosley Field [Cincinnati] and Braves Field [Boston], where, if it weren't caught, it would have been a double off the fence. That's the whole National League. In the American League, it would have been an uncatchable double at Fenway Park [Boston] and catchable in St. Louis, Cleveland, Comiskey, Detroit, Philadelphia, Washington, and Yankee Stadium in New York.

No matter. Regardless of whether Thomson's fly ball would have been a home run nowhere but the Polo Grounds, it was the Polo Grounds where it was hit.

But the game above all others that best demonstrates the vagaries of the Polo Grounds—and how the stadium could taketh away as well as giveth—may have been the opener of the 1954 World Series between the Cleveland Indians and New York Giants. Cleveland came into the series as the favorites after having set an American League single-season record by winning 111 games. However, they would win no more.

With the first game tied, 2–2, Larry Doby of the Indians walked to open the eighth inning and went to second on an infield hit by Al Rosen. Left-hander Don Liddle was brought in to face Vic Wertz, Cleveland's powerful first baseman. On a two-strike pitch, Wertz drilled a tremendous drive to center field. Willie Mays turned and ran back toward the fence to the right of the alcove. Mays stuck out his glove and, three steps in front of the warning track, caught the fly over his right shoulder. The catch was remarkable, but so was what he did next. Mays was so far away that if he couldn't get the ball in quickly, Doby would have had a chance to tag up and score all the way from second base. Mays spun and heaved the ball back toward the infield as he fell to the ground. Doby was able to get no farther than third on the play and was stranded there by the subsequent Cleveland batters. Thanks to Mays's great play, the game remained deadlocked.

In the last of the tenth inning, with the score still tied, 2–2, the Giants put runners on first and second with one out. Dusty Rhodes, a left-handed batter, pinch hit for Monte Irvin and lifted a fly to right field. Right fielder Dave Pope drifted over toward the line but quickly came up against the fence. He leaped but the ball came down beyond his reach, into the first row of fans for a game-winning home run. Dusty Rhodes won the game with a home run that traveled barely 260 feet while, two innings earlier, Vic Wertz had sent one well in excess of 400 feet that was nothing more than a long fly out.

The exact distance Mays was from home plate when he made the catch on Wertz's drive has prompted a great deal of debate among baseball historians. The most popular notion puts the catch approximately 440 feet from home plate, although many scholars claim it was no more than 405 to 410 feet away. Enough still photos and film footage exist to make it possible to mark the location where Mays made the catch. However, there is disagreement over how far this spot was from home plate, which points out the confusion regarding the distances to center field at the Polo Grounds. The marked distances on diagrams as well as within the stadium changed over the years. For much of the park's history, a 483-foot marker was attached to the clubhouse wall in center field (at the back of the alcove). By the 1960s, the length was listed at 475. At other times, 505 feet was the distance cited. Phil Lowry said he was never able to clear up the question of why the distances changed. "It could have been due to remeasurements or a slight shift of home plate's location," he wrote in *Green Cathedrals.* "Or it could have been a measurement to the base of the Eddie Grant Memorial. In the Giants' time, reading from left to right, the markers read 315, 360, 414, 447, 455, 483, 455, 483, 455, 449, 395, 338, 294. In the Mets' time [in the 1960s], they read 306, 405, 475, 405, 281. The foul lines were never marked."

Dusty Rhodes provided more heroics in the second game of the 1954 World Series. He pinch hit for Monte Irvin again, this time in the fifth inning, and singled home the tying run. With the Giants ahead, 2–1, in the seventh, Rhodes capped the game's scoring with another home run to right. The Giants won the next two games to finish off the Indians, but the first game remained the focal point of the series sweep. Mays's catch and Rhodes's home run became staples of newsreel footage and baseball highlight films.

Another Game 1 legacy was a book entitled *A Day in the Bleachers* by Arnold Hano, who chronicled the hours he spent in the center-field bleachers of the Polo Grounds that day. In the book Hano provided vivid descriptions of batting practice and other pregame events along with a detailed play-by-play account of the game, with special emphasis on the game-saving catch by Mays. *A Day in the Bleachers* is often cited as the first adult baseball book. "Previous books by authors such as Fred Lieb and John Tunis were directed toward young readers," stated Ted Hathaway, a librarian and one of the creators of the Research in Baseball Index (a massive catalog and database of baseball literature). "*A Day in the Bleachers* was the first book of its kind that was written for adults."

The different New York baseball teams during these years seemed to produce distinct types of followers. Fred Stein contrasted the typical Giant fans with the zany characters who were regulars at Ebbets Field as well as with Yankee fans, who he said were "far less demonstrative and emotionally involved. My recollection of the typical Yankee fan of that era is of a relatively quiet citizen, watching the game with casual detachment, with complete confidence in a satisfactory outcome regardless of temporary setbacks. . . . Giant fans were a different, more sophisticated, breed. Not for us were the emotional excesses or theatrics of the Dodger fan or the quiet calm of the Yankee adherents."

But there were more than issues of personality to determine who rooted for whom. For some, it was a matter of geography (particularly in Brooklyn, where residence in that borough normally meant allegiance to the Dodgers), but this wasn't always the case.

Larry "Moose" Stubing and Grover "Deacon" Jones are examples of fans who grew up in the New York City area in the 1940s and 1950s. Both went on to careers in professional baseball as players (with brief tenures in the major leagues) and later as coaches and scouts. Stubing grew up in the Bronx, home of Yankee Stadium, although he identified himself primarily as a Giants fan. "I don't know why," he said. "Maybe the Polo Grounds was the stadium my dad took me to first." Jones, who was raised in White Plains in suburban Westchester County, provided a clearer explanation for why he became a Dodger fan. "It was Jackie Robinson," he said, referring to the player who broke baseball's color barrier at the time Jones was entering his teens.

Both Stubing and Jones spent time in all the New York stadiums, sometimes as spectators and sometimes as players on high school and area all star teams. They also played the game they loved in any other setting that worked—whether it be a vacant lot or the middle of a street. Often they were forced to improvise in terms of players and equipment. "We'd play all day," recalled Jones, adding that "kids today have no imagination. They can't play unless they have 18 players [enough for two full teams]." Jones and Stubing would manage with far smaller numbers, even to the point of drawing the outline of a strike zone on the wall of a handball court and pitching to an imaginary batter. Balls were kept in service for long periods by being wrapped with tape. If a regulation ball wasn't available, a tennis ball could suffice if the fuzz was burned off. "Tennis balls were a lot fuzzier then," Stubing explained, "and all that fuzz would slow the ball down."

On the sandlots and in high school, Stubing, who is white, and Jones, who is black, played in groups that were racially diverse. Stubing said the neighborhoods he was familiar with in New York City were broken up more on the lines of nationality or other ethnic divisions rather than by color. "There were Italian or German or Jewish neighborhoods more than any that were black or white," he remembered. Neither Jones nor Stubing gave much thought to race relations until they entered pro ball and got a dose of Southern segregation—Jones on his first trip to Florida for spring training with the Chicago White Sox organization and Stubing with his first pro team in the Georgia-Florida League.

The times were changing—as the stories of Stubing and Jones illustrate—and the 1950s turned into a most tumultuous period for fans of the National League baseball teams in New York. Reports of the possible abandonment of the Polo Grounds had begun in the early 1950s. In the September 1953 *Sport* magazine, Jack Orr wrote, "There have been recent rumors that the Giants, at the expiration of their current lease in 1962, will turn the tables and become tenants of the Yankees." That fall, planner Robert Moses—the "master builder" of New York City—suggested that the Giants make the move even sooner so the Polo Grounds could be torn down and used for public housing.

Soon the uncertain future of the Polo Grounds was casting shadows on the future of the Giants in New York. The team wasn't averse to leaving the Polo Grounds. Parking had always been a problem, the stadium was becoming rundown, and the neighborhood was also deteriorating. (Before the start of an Independence Day doubleheader in 1950, a fan in the upper grandstand of the Polo Grounds was even killed by a stray bullet fired from outside the stadium.)

Moving into Yankee Stadium was one alternative. A new stadium, built by the city, was one that appealed even more to owner Horace Stoneham. Paul Ferrante, a sports memorabilia collector who became an expert on the Polo Grounds while tracking down remnants of the stadium, said a 470,000-square-foot tract of land in Manhattan, then occupied by the New York Central Railroad, was being considered for a new stadium in the spring of 1956.

Bounded by West End Highway, 60th Street, West End Avenue, and 72nd Street, a triple-decked, roofed stadium would be built on stilts over the railroad tracks. The project—estimated at $20 million—never got beyond the proposal stage.

By the following year, Stoneham was talking about a city-owned stadium in Queens, near the Bronx-Whitestone Bridge. He was also making it clear that the Giants were no longer limiting their options to New York City.

Meanwhile, similar threats were being made in Brooklyn. Dodgers owner Walter O'Malley, also wanting a new stadium, was viewing the fertile territory on the West Coast as a possible place to play. In turn, Stoneham looked in the same direction. In late May of 1957, National League officials gave Brooklyn and New York the go-ahead to negotiate for a move to Los Angeles and San Francisco, respectively. Not long after, Stoneham said, "This is definitely our last year in New York."

Stoneham was also considering Minneapolis, where the Giants had their top minor league team, as a possible home. (The Minneapolis Millers were by this time playing their games in a new suburban stadium that had a cantilever design, free of posts that could obstruct views. The Minneapolis firm of Thorshov and Cerny, which had designed the stadium, had visited other stadiums across the country, looking specifically for defects they should avoid. The main defect they found in several of the stadiums, including the Polo Grounds, was the supporting posts that blocked the view of various parts of the playing field for many spectators. The modern stadium gave Midwest residents hope that they could lure the Giants to Minnesota.)

In the end, however, Stoneham opted for California, along with O'Malley and the Dodgers. The news left area fans in a state of melancholy. With the National League teams moving out, New York would be left with only the Yankees, hardly an acceptable team for Dodger and Giant loyalists to rally behind.

The ends came in September of 1957. On Sunday, September 29—just five days after the Dodgers had played their final game at Ebbets Field—the New York Giants brought their history to a close. The crowd of 11,606 that turned out for the final game wasn't large considering that it was the final game of the New York Giants as well as what many presumed would be the last baseball game for the Polo Grounds. However, it was still well above what the Giants had been averaging that season, and it included a number of special guests. Blanche McGraw, widow of the Giants' legendary manager, showed up, as did former New York players Rube Marquard, George "Hooks" Wiltse, Moose McCormick, George "Kiddo" Davis, Rosy Ryan, Carl Hubbell, Red

Murray, Hans Lobert, Willard Marshall, Sid Gordon, Prince Hal Schumacher, Billy Jurges, Monte Irvin, Buddy Kerr, and 86-year-old Jack Doyle, who had played for and managed the Giants in the 1890s. Another octogenarian, George Levy, was on hand to repeat his earlier practice from the pre-electronic era of announcing the lineups through a megaphone.

Manager Bill Rigney showed a nostalgic side by loading his lineup with players from the pennant-winning teams of 1951 and 1954. Don Mueller, Willie Mays, Dusty Rhodes, Bobby Thomson, Whitey Lockman, Wes Westrum, and Johnny Antonelli were among the starters for New York. The opponents, the Pittsburgh Pirates, weren't as sentimental about the event as they pounded the Giants, 9–1. The game, and a rich slice of history, came to an end at 4:35 P.M. when Dusty Rhodes—one of the heroes of the 1954 World Series—grounded to Pirates shortstop Dick Groat. Before Groat's throw had even settled into the glove of first baseman Frank Thomas, fans were leaping over fences and pouring onto the fields.

The Giants and Pirates tore across the Polo Grounds outfield toward the clubhouses, getting out of the path of the onrushing fans, many of who were determined to come away with a souvenir. One group went to work on extricating home plate from its mooring, while others scooped up the bases.

In center field, the orange-lettered green sign reading "483 FEET" was pulled back and forth in an attempt to work it loose. Guards intervened before anyone could take the sign as a keepsake, but they weren't as successful at keeping the Eddie Grant plaque in place. Looters were able to pry the plaque off the stone monument, although police did nab the thieves.

Many fans were content to station themselves in the alcove and hope to get a glimpse of their departing heros through the clubhouse windows. They chanted Willie Mays's name, but when Mays didn't appear, they began calling instead for Horace Stoneham—although for entirely different reasons. "We want Stoneham! We want Stoneham!" they bellowed, then—to make sure their intentions weren't misunderstood—modified the chant to "We want Stoneham—with a rope around his neck!" The crowd on the field finally had enough and left, but some remained in the stands. Fittingly, the last to leave—still clutching a bouquet of roses that Rigney had presented to her before the game—was Blanche McGraw.

National League baseball had abandoned New York City—but the two ballparks, Ebbets Field and the Polo Grounds—remained for several years and were used for a variety of events. Ebbets Field was finally knocked down in February of 1960; the Polo Grounds not only lived on but had a rebirth of sorts.

First, it absorbed a soccer team that had been playing at Ebbets Field. It also obtained a new football tenant, the New York Titans (later renamed the Jets) of the American Football League in 1960. And, by 1962, even baseball had returned. Ironically, by this time, the death warrant for the Polo Grounds had been issued, and it was clear that the stadium was in its final years.

Baseball—the primary sport associated with the Polo Grounds—came back when New York was granted a National League franchise. The process began in 1959, when the Continental League was formed as a potential third major league. New York was one of the cities designated for a franchise in the new league, which ended up disbanding (before ever actually operating) after receiving agreement from both major leagues to absorb some of its teams, including New York.

It meant that, starting in 1962, New York would have a team in the National League again, this one taking the name of its American Association predecessor from the 1880s, the Metropolitans (although this team would be known simply as the Mets). Part of the bargain, however, was that the Mets would have a new stadium. In January of 1961, the New York City Board of Estimate approved plans to build a stadium in Flushing Meadow (a portion of the borough of Queens). The stadium wouldn't be ready until at least 1963, which meant the Mets would have to find another place to play in their initial season. They thus sought permission from the Yankees to share Yankee Stadium with them for a year.

The month of March 1961 was an active one in terms of issues related to the Mets, including a scare that left the future of the team in doubt. On Wednesday, March 15, the New York State Assembly—which had to pass a bill authorizing the city to finance and build the stadium and lease it to the Mets—fell well short of the two-thirds vote needed for approval. Without passage of the bill, there would be no stadium, and without the stadium, there would be no Mets. The setback didn't last long, though. A number of dissenters were persuaded overnight to change their votes, and the next day the measure necessary for a new stadium to be built was passed by a vote of 119–17.

That crisis out of the way, the long-term plans for the Mets were solidified. Short-term plans, however, remained in limbo as the Yankees made it clear they had no intention of allowing the Mets to share their stadium.

That left the Polo Grounds as the remaining option for the Mets. Although the stadium had continued to be used for other events after the departure of the Giants, baseball hadn't been played there since 1957, and a great deal of work would have to be done to make it suitable for a baseball tenant again. The Mets were willing to incur the expenses for the necessary renovations, but a larger problem loomed.

On March 9, 1961, the New York City Board of Estimate had doomed the Polo Grounds with a decision to demolish the stadium to allow the New York City Housing Authority to erect a low-rent housing project—consisting of four 30-story towers to house more than 1,600 families—on the site. (The decision wasn't made with the blessing of the Coogan heirs, who still owned the site. Jay Coogan, who fought the takeover attempt by the city, had earlier appeared before the City Planning Commission with a proposal to convert the stadium into a covered "sports palace," one with a price tag of $45 million. The commission rejected Coogan's plan, though, stating that the need for low-income housing was greater. The value of the land was hotly contested by both sides and wasn't resolved until a decision was issued by the New York Court of Appeals in November 1967, more than three years after the stadium had been razed.)

Since the New York Titans of the American Football League already had a lease to use the Polo Grounds through the end of 1961, it meant that the city couldn't proceed with its plans for a housing project on the site until 1962 at the earliest. Understanding the plight of the New York Mets, who needed a temporary home, the city further delayed the housing project for at least another year.

This was good news for New York baseball fans, particularly those who had learned to loathe the Yankees and had been hungry for another National League team to cheer for. (Some Brooklyn fans, though, still associated the Polo Grounds with the once-hated Giants and made it known they would not attend a Mets game until the team's new stadium, in the neutral territory of Queens, was ready.)

The Mets proceeded with work to get the Polo Grounds ready for baseball and spent more than $300,000 on the project, a huge sum considering that they were planning on using the stadium only for a year. The refurbishing included painting of the fences and stands, replacement of lamps and reflectors in the lighting towers, installation of an electronic scoreboard that stretched across the clubhouse in center field, and construction of a private cocktail club and restaurant known as the Met Lounge. Advertising signs once again adorned the outfield fences.

The biggest project, though, dealt with the playing area itself. (Some of the events held in the Polo Grounds after the departure of the Giants were tough on the turf. One such event was midget auto racing, which was run on an asphalt track that had been constructed on the field.) The grounds crew plowed the entire field, brought in topsoil, and spent a month grading the area before installing more than 130,000 square feet of sod. The face-lift of the Polo Grounds was a massive effort but one that was well worth it. New Yorkers were excited about their new team, and, for their initial season, the Mets rang up the largest sales ever for season tickets at the Polo Grounds.

The Polo Grounds' previous tenant, the Giants, had been one of the most storied teams in baseball history. The Mets established their identity at the Polo Grounds in an entirely different way. In a rather perverse turn of events, though, the ineptness and futility of the Mets proved as big a hit with the fans as the legacy of greatness of the Giants.

Banners and placards decorated the Polo Grounds during the Mets' tenure, paying homage to the players and their manager, Casey Stengel. Stengel had managed the Yankees from 1949 through 1960, leading the team to 10 pennants and 7 World Series titles in that 12-year span. Still, his earlier reputation for buffoonery and his strange linguistic style (a language known as "Stengelese") meshed nicely with the zaniness that was Mets baseball in the early 1960s.

The real darling of the Polo Grounds (albeit an often-booed darling) and the man who epitomized not just the losses, but the way the team lost, was first baseman Marv Throneberry. Stories abound about Throneberry's bungling at bat, in the field, and on the base paths, but the one that best sums up Throneberry, and the Mets, occurred at the Polo Grounds in the first game of a doubleheader against the Chicago Cubs on Sunday, June 17, 1962. The Mets had a runner on first base when Throneberry hit a deep fly to right field and ended up at third base with an apparent triple. However, he was called out on appeal for missing first base on his journey around the bases. Casey Stengel came out to argue—to no avail, of course—and was perturbed by the lack of support he got in the rhubarb from his first-base coach, Cookie Lavagetto. On his way back to the dugout, Stengel expressed his disapproval to Lavagetto, who revealed why he had been hesitant to join the argument: "Marv missed second base, too." (When the next batter, Charlie Neal, homered, Stengel came out of the dugout and pointed to each of the four bases as Neal made his way around the diamond.)

These strange scenes occurred in the last of the first inning in the game against the Cubs. In the top of the inning, Chicago's Lou Brock had homered into the center-field bleachers. His drive, off the Mets' Al Jackson, hit the top of the fence to the right of the large batter's eye and bounced into the bleachers. The next day, Hank Aaron of the Milwaukee Braves connected off Jay Hook for another blast into the center-field bleachers, this one a grand-slam home run to the left of the batter's eye on the left side of the alcove. Brock's and Aaron's homers were only the third and fourth to reach the bleachers since the 1922 renovation of the Polo Grounds, Joe Adcock of the Braves having performed the feat in 1953 and Luke Easter of the Homestead Grays in 1948.

It was normal that the moments of greatness at the Polo Grounds in 1962 were provided by the visiting teams. The Mets finished the season with 120 losses—the most in the majors since 1899—out of 160 games, for a losing percentage of .750.

As highlights and lowlights punctuated the 1962 season, construction on the stadium in Flushing was underway. The 1962 Mets program said: "When the stadium opens in 1963, it will have a seating capacity of 55,000 which will eventually be raised to 85,000. At the time of the installation of the additional 30,000 seats, the stadium will be domed in so that it will be an all-weather stadium and rain checks will be a thing of the past."

Neither the additional 30,000 seats—nor the dome—were ever added to the new stadium. There were already enough problems with keeping construction of the basic design on track. Hampered by labor disputes and problems with subcontractors, the project was behind schedule in August 1962 and slowed further by harsh weather over the winter of 1962–63. Still, when the Mets concluded their regular season in 1962, they fully expected to be in their new home for the opening of the next season. In fact, the *New York Times* headline of Monday, September 24, 1962, read, "Mets Beat Cubs, 2–1, in Farewell to Baseball at the Polo Grounds." A crowd of 10,304 attended what they thought would be the stadium's final baseball game.

However, the Polo Grounds received still another reprieve. When it became clear the Flushing stadium wouldn't be ready, the Mets resigned themselves to at least another partial season beneath Coogan's Bluff. It turned out to be a full season at the Polo Grounds, with the final game played before only 1,752 fans—the smallest crowd to see the Mets at that location. "Maybe the fact that there had been two previous 'last games' [the 1957 Giants finale and final home game in 1962] at the Polo Grounds took a bit from the occasion," wrote Gordon S. White, Jr., in the *New York Times.* "It is hoped that no more Mets games will be played at the Polo Grounds—if only to put an end to the string of finales."

This was the final finale, with the Philadelphia Phillies beating the Mets, 5–1. The end came at 4:21 P.M.. on Wednesday, September 18, 1963, with New York's Ted Schreiber hitting into a double play to end the game. Jim Hickman provided the Mets' only run in the fourth inning with a home run, the last ever hit at the Polo Grounds.

In January of 1964, the Mets moved their offices out of the Polo Grounds and into the new stadium in Queens, which became known as Shea Stadium. That April, demolition of the Polo Grounds started with the same wrecking ball that had been used four years earlier on Ebbets Field. The wrecking crew wore Giants jerseys and tipped their hard hats to the venerable stadium as they began the dismantling. It took a crew of 60 workers more than four months to bring the venerable structure down.

New Yorkers in general seemed to witness the end of the Polo Grounds with a sense of detachment rather than nostalgia. "The Polo Grounds was a magnificent relic of the past that thrived on its own individual characteristics, which some of us at the time did not fully appreciate," wrote George Tinker, a longtime fan, more than 20 years after the stadium closed.

However, Roger Angell, the celebrated writer for the *New Yorker*, had earlier provided a fitting eulogy for the Polo Grounds with an article written in the spring of 1963:

> The Polo Grounds, which is in the last few months of its disreputable life, is a vast assemblage of front stoops and rusty fire escapes. . . . Old-timers know and love every corner of the crazy, crowded, proud old neighborhood: the last-row walkup flats in the outermost lower grandstands, where one must peer through girders and pigeon nests for a glimpse of green; the little protruding step at the foot of each aisle in the upper deck that trips up the unwary beer-balancer on his way back to his seat; the outfield bull pens, each with its slanting shanty roof, beneath which the relief pitchers sit motionless, with their arms folded and their legs extended, like so many park bums; and the good box seats just on the curve of the upper deck in short right and short left—front windows on the street, where one can watch the arching fall of a weak fly ball and know in advance, like one who sees a street accident in the making, that it will collide with that ridiculous, dangerous upper tier for another home run.

Angell concluded by envisioning a conversation that might take place a few years later among fans who used to come to the Polo Grounds: "Funny, I was thinking of the old place today. Remember how jammed we used to be back there? Remember how hot and noisy it was? I wouldn't move back there for anything, and anyway it's all torn down now, but, you know, we sure were happy in those days."

For many years advertisements adorned the walls of the Polo Grounds.

Fans arriving via the elevated line on Eighth Avenue could enter the Polo Grounds under the right-field stands. Collection of Michael Frank

Yankee Stadium is shown in the foreground, with the Polo Grounds across the Harlem River, 1950s or 1960s. The Putnam Bridge, near center field of the Polo Grounds, no longer exists, although the Macombs Dam Bridge at left still stands. The toughest part of the walk between the stadiums was the climb up a 135-step stairway from Coogan's Hollow to the 155th Street viaduct. The vacant lot to the left of the stadium was the site of a nineteenth-century Polo Grounds.

Baseball's most memorable moment occurred at the Polo Grounds on October 3, 1951: Bobby Thomson's three-run homer in the last of the ninth to give the Giants the National League pennant over the Brooklyn Dodgers.

Another great moment at the Polo Grounds was Willie Mays's catch of Vic Wertz's drive in the opening game of the 1954 World Series.

The repair shops for the subway and elevated cars on the north side of the Polo Grounds were demolished in the 1940s and replaced by the Colonial Park housing project, shown here. Transcendental Graphics

Willie Mays batting at the Polo Grounds in 1957.

The end of the New York Giants occurs as the final out is made in the last game of the 1957 season. The next year, the Giants were playing in San Francisco. It was thought at the time that baseball would never again be played in the Polo Grounds. AP/Wide World Photos

Baseball returned to the Polo Grounds in 1962 with the arrival of the New York Mets. Collection of Michael Frank

The Polo Grounds underwent another face-lift with the coming of the Mets. Among other things, advertisements were back on the outfield fences.

• FOOTBALL •

POLO GROUNDS

First Game of the League Season

Sunday, Oct. 16th – 2.30 p.m.

CHRIS "RED" CAGLE and the

New York Football Giants

vs.

BENNY FRIEDMAN and his

Brooklyn Dodgers

1925 • EIGHTH SEASON • 1932

Baseball wasn't the only sport at the Polo Grounds.

STRIKES BALLS
N.Y.
A.B.
VIS.
74
53
49
20

President Woodrow Wilson was among the spectators for the first Army-Navy game to be played at the Polo Grounds, on November 29, 1913. Collection of Michael Frank

Army football was a big attraction at the Polo Grounds during the 1940s. The Sporting News

The Polo Grounds was abandoned after the 1963 baseball and football seasons.

The Polo Grounds finally came down in 1964. Demolition began in April with the same wrecking ball that had been used on Ebbets Field in Brooklyn four years earlier.

CHAPTER NINE

Boxing to Buffalo Bill

THE FINAL BASEBALL GAME WASN'T ACTUALLY THE FINAL EVENT AT THE Polo Grounds. The official end to the stadium came with an American Football League game between the Buffalo Bills and New York Jets (formerly the Titans) on Saturday, December 14, 1963. Buffalo quarterback Jack Kemp, who entered the game in place of starting quarterback Daryle Lamonica, led a second-half surge that gave Buffalo a 19–10 win over the Jets before a dismal crowd of 5,826. Eventually, in their new stadium, the Jets would become a hit attraction, but their years at the Polo Grounds—whether as the Jets or as the Titans—were spent playing in front of mostly empty seats.

The final home game of the 1962 season for the Titans produced so little interest that team owner Harry Wismer reportedly had an aide running through the adjacent neighborhood, shouting an offer that all kids would be admitted free of charge. Wismer was concerned about playing in a huge stadium that looked so empty. His ploy didn't work. The paid attendance was listed at 3,828 (lowest in American Football League history), but most agreed that the stands contained fewer than 1,000 spectators.

Although the American Football League had trouble getting fans to come to the Polo Grounds, the National Football League (NFL) did have more success during the 31-year period that the New York Giants (the football Giants) used the stadium as their home. Until the formation of the Giants in 1925, the NFL had been little more than a loose collection of teams occupying mostly small towns in the Midwest. But even in New York, the NFL struggled through most of the 1925 season. The turning point came in early December, although the impetus for the excitement had nothing to do with the Giants; rather, it was the appearance of a visiting player that caused more than 70,000 fans, a new NFL record, to pass through the turnstiles of the Polo Grounds.

The player was Red Grange, who only two weeks before had completed his legendary collegiate football career at the University of Illinois. Along with Notre Dame football coach Knute Rockne, boxer Jack Dempsey, and Yankees slugger Babe Ruth, Grange (nicknamed the "Galloping Ghost") helped define the 1920s as the golden age of sports in the twentieth century.

In the 1920s, college football commanded greater interest than the professional game, which was struggling to establish an identity and a place in the hearts of football fans. While today the next step for college stars is the National Football League, such was not the case in the league's early years. George Halas, owner of the Chicago Bears, recognized the boost a player like Grange could give to the NFL and made it his mission to get the Galloping Ghost into a Bears uniform.

Grange and his manager, C. C. Pyle, were well aware of his drawing power and agreed to a professional contract only after Halas consented to pay him a percentage of the gate receipts from games he played in. The day after Grange played his last college game, he announced his intentions to turn professional with Chicago. Giants owner Tim Mara—who had hoped to sign Grange himself—immediately arranged a game with the Bears for the Polo Grounds on Sunday, December 6. For the first time, there was a run on tickets for a Giants football game.

The stadium was filled the day of the game, and Grange did not disappoint the New York fans, even though his outstanding play brought to an end a seven-game winning streak by the Giants. Grange played the entire first quarter and part of the second before retiring for the rest of the half and all of the third quarter. In the fourth quarter, New York trailed, 13–7, but the fans were more intent on seeing Grange's return to the gridiron than they were on a Giants comeback. They chanted, "We want Grange!" until finally Halas accommodated their wishes and sent his star back in. Soon after, Grange intercepted a New York pass and returned it 35 yards for a touchdown to seal the Chicago victory. In addition to the interception return, Grange rushed for 53 yards on 11 plays from scrimmage; threw three forward passes, two of which were completed for a total 32 yards; caught one pass for 23 yards; and returned two kicks for a total of 13 yards. Those in attendance at the Polo

Grounds agreed that Grange was well worth his share of the gate receipts, which came to approximately $30,000.

Eventually, the New York Giants were able to produce highlights of their own at the Polo Grounds. One came in the December 1934 league title game between the Giants and the heavily favored Bears, who had finished the regular season with a record of 13 wins and no losses. The morning of the game, Robert F. Kelley of the *New York Times* predicted, "Granted good playing conditions, there is the strong probability that some of the most advanced football the country has ever seen will be played." However, the playing conditions were anything but good. An overnight rain followed by subfreezing temperatures turned the Polo Grounds gridiron into almost a sheet of ice. On the morning of the game, Giants captain Ray Flaherty suggested that the team try to find rubber-soled shoes, knowing that cleats would be virtually useless on the frozen turf. Coming up with enough sneakers to outfit an entire football team on a Sunday in December wasn't easy; however, the Giants were able to get through to the Manhattan College athletic department, which agreed to loan them basketball shoes.

The sneakers didn't arrive until after the game had started, and the Giants weren't able to change into them until halftime. By this point, they were trailing the Bears, 10–3, and fell further behind in the third quarter, as Chicago produced another field goal. Finally, in the fourth quarter, the improved footing paid off, as the Giants stormed back with 27 unanswered points to win, 30–13. Bronko Nagurski, Chicago's great fullback who had scored the Bears' only touchdown of the game, thought the shoes made the difference in the game for the Giants. "I think the sneakers gave them [the Giants] and edge in that last half," said Nagurski, "for they were able to cut back when they were running with the ball, and we couldn't cut with them."

Another championship game at the Polo Grounds didn't even involve a New York team. The 1936 NFL title game between the Boston Redskins and Green Bay Packers was scheduled for Boston. But the Boston franchise was in the process of being moved to Washington, D.C., and team owner George Preston Marshall, unhappy with the lack of fans who had been coming to games in Boston, shifted the title game to the Polo Grounds. A crowd of 29,545 mostly nonpartisan fans watched the Packers beat the Redskins, 21–6.

Three other NFL title games were played at the Polo Grounds. The Giants beat the Packers, 23–17, in 1938, winning on a third-quarter touchdown reception by Hank Soar, who later became an American League umpire. In 1944 it was the Packers who beat the Giants, 14–7. This was also the last game for New York tackle Al Blozis, who went from the gridiron to combat in World War II and disappeared in a snowstorm in France in January 1945. Over 58,000 fans watched the 1946 NFL title game—the last one played in the Polo Grounds—in which the Bears beat the Giants, 24–14.

In addition to the title games, the Pro All Star Game (now the Pro Bowl) was played at the Polo Grounds on January 4, 1942. All the previous All Star Games had been played in Los Angeles. However, with Pearl Harbor having been bombed less than the month before, the game was moved because of fears of a Japanese invasion of the West Coast. The 1941 NFL champion Chicago Bears beat a collection of All Stars from other teams, 35–24. (In July 1942, the baseball All Star Game was played at the Polo Grounds. The Los Angeles Coliseum is the only other stadium to have hosted all star games for both the National Football League and major league baseball in the same calendar year.)

The football Giants played at the Polo Grounds through the 1955 season before moving their home games to Yankee Stadium. Team owner Wellington Mara cited the uncertainty of the future of the baseball Giants, and subsequently, the Polo Grounds, as the reason for the switch in stadiums.

Professional football games had been played at the Polo Grounds before the advent of the New York Giants—or the National Football League, for that matter. On Saturday, December 4, 1920, the Polo Grounds hosted a game between the Canton Bulldogs and Buffalo All-Americans of the American Professional Football Association (APFA), the forerunner of the NFL. Approximately 15,000 fans were at the game, attracted mainly by the chance to see Jim Thorpe, Canton's captain and halfback. There was little offense in the game—only three first downs, all by Buffalo—but Thorpe put on a show by doing all the punting and kicking for Canton, including a drop-kick for a field goal that gave the Bulldogs a 3–0 lead in the third quarter. Thorpe later had a 40-yard punt return, although Canton couldn't capitalize on the play. Buffalo came up with a touchdown in the third quarter and hung on for a 7–3 win. The closing moments of the game featured three long pass attempts by Thorpe—all in excess of 30 yards—to his star end, Joe Guyon. All were incomplete.

In 1921, New York had a team of its own in the APFA—sort of. The New York Brickley's Giants, named after team organizer and coach Charley Brickley, played just two games against other APFA opponents. One of them was at the Polo Grounds, on Saturday, December 3, and it generated little interest. The Cleveland Tigers beat Brickley's Giants, 17–0, in front of 3,000 fans, a gathering that, according to the *New York Times*, "contented itself with quietly watching the game over the tops of its well-buttoned overcoats, emerging now and then to laugh at the grotesqueness of some former star vainly trying to hit the line or run the ends as in days of yore."

Clearly, college football enjoyed far greater distinction nationally than the professional game at the time. This was the case in New York as well. Although pro football produced some memorable moments at the Polo Grounds, it was the college game that had a greater presence there. Area colleges, as well as some schools from far away, scheduled games at the stadium. For a time, the Polo Grounds served as the home for Dartmouth College of Hanover, New Hampshire.

Beginning in 1913, the Polo Grounds also became the regular site of the annual Army-Navy game for many years. Except for a five-year span between 1894 and 1898, Army and Navy had met on the gridiron every year since 1890, and, except for one year when the teams met in Princeton, New Jersey, the game had always been played in Philadelphia. The shift to New York City resulted in a huge increase in interest and prestige for the rivalry. The first game in New York, played on Saturday, November 29, 1913, was also the first football game in the Polo Grounds since the stadium had been rebuilt in 1911. President Woodrow Wilson attended the game, as did his entire cabinet as well as congressional representatives from every state. They and the 42,000 other spectators saw Army upset the previously unbeaten Navy team by a score of 22–9.

Following a 1939 game between Indiana and Rice (the latter school located in Houston, Texas), 64 college teams had played at the Polo Grounds since the 1890s. "Nearly a tenth of all grid outfits listed in the intercollegiate guide have had their representatives performing at one time or another on the historic lot under Coogan's Bluff," reported the *New York Sun* on October 26, 1939.

The college team most closely associated with the Polo Grounds was Notre Dame University of South Bend, Indiana. According to Murray Sperber in *Shake Down the Thunder: The Creation of Notre Dame Football*, Notre Dame coach Jesse Harper was invited to play at the Polo Grounds in 1915. However, even though Harper was trying to establish a national schedule, he turned down the offer. However, Harper's assistant, Knute Rockne, kept the offer in mind, and, after becoming the team's head coach, sought to use the Polo Grounds for Notre Dame's annual contest with Army in 1920. This time it was Army—fearful that such a game might undermine its Polo Grounds rivalry with Navy—who balked.

Three years later, both teams agreed to move their contest to the Polo Grounds. But now there was another hitch. The baseball Giants were in the

World Series, making the Polo Grounds unavailable for football. The 1923 game between Notre Dame and Army was played at Ebbets Field in Brooklyn.

Finally, in 1924, the two teams met at the Polo Grounds for the first time, on Saturday, October 18. Notre Dame had one of its best teams ever that year, led by an all-senior backfield of Jim Crowley, Don Miller, Elmer Layden, and Harry Stuhldreher. The quartet performed admirably in Notre Dame's 13–7 win over Army, prompting Grantland Rice of the *New York Herald Tribune* to compose one of the most famous leads in the history of sports journalism:

> Outlined against a blue-gray October sky, the Four Horsemen rode again. In dramatic lore they were known as Famine, Pestilence, Destruction and Death. These are only aliases. Their real names are Stuhldreher, Miller, Crowley and Layden. They formed the crest of the South Bend cyclone before which another fighting Army football team was swept over the precipice at the Polo Grounds yesterday afternoon as 55,000 spectators peered down on the bewildering panorama on the green plain below.

Thanks to Rice's prose—and the perspicacity of George Strickler, the school's student press assistant, who the following week arranged for a photo of the backfield members mounted on horses—the Four Horsemen were christened and a phenomenon launched. "In the history of college football," concluded Sperber in *Shake Down the Thunder*, "coaches have assembled many outstanding backfields, but none are better known than the Four Horsemen of Notre Dame. Grantland Rice and his colleagues proved that words are more powerful than the most bruising football 'hit' and that words can manufacture apparent realities far different from what actually happened."

The largest throngs ever to witness sporting events at the Polo Grounds, though, weren't for either baseball or football. Boxing matches required less space than either game, leaving more room on the field for spectators. The top crowd at the Polo Grounds, more than 82,000, was for the September 1923 title fight in which Jack Dempsey—despite being knocked out of the ring in the first round—defended his championship with a second-round knockout of the "Wild Bull of the Pampas," Luis Firpo. The Dempsey-Firpo brawl capped the first season of boxing at the Polo Grounds and was the fifth championship bout held there that year. (The first Polo Grounds match was held in June 1923 with Eugene Criqui knocking out Johnny Kilbane in the sixth round of the main event for the world featherweight title.) Jersey Jones, in an 1964 article for *The Ring* magazine published after the demolition of the Polo Grounds, wrote, "That eventful summer of '23 established the Polo Grounds as a popular center of major outdoor ring attractions."

One of the most famous bouts at the Polo Grounds was the June 1941 heavyweight title fight between champion Joe Louis and challenger Billy Conn. This was the event that prompted the prefight verbal sparring capped by Louis's pithy claim that Conn "can run but he can't hide."

For the first 12 rounds, Conn had no need to hide. He was outboxing Louis, and many observers felt all that Conn had to do was keep his distance in the final three rounds to receive a clear-cut decision and the world title. Instead, Conn went for the knockout, with disastrous results. In the thirteenth round, Conn left himself open for what the *New York Times* reported as "one dangerous blow to a vital point." The *Times* account added that Louis "whipped home though the opening with a right to the jaw. The blow landed high, but it was a powerful one. . . . He [Louis] leaped in savagely, thudding home with both hands under a crushing fire. Conn fell under the barrage, a right to the jaw as a final thrust."

Later in the year, Louis again successfully defended his title at the Polo Grounds with a knockout of Lou Nova. In June 1960, the Polo Grounds was the site of Floyd Patterson's knockout of Ingemar Johansson, allowing Patterson to regain the heavyweight title that Johansson had taken from him the year before. It was also the last boxing card held at the Polo Grounds.

In between the Criqui-Kilbane match of June 1923 and the Patterson-Johansson bout 37 years later, the Polo Grounds hosted boxing matches that included Gene Tunney, Georges Carpentier, Mickey Walker, Tommy Gibbons, Jack Dempsey, Kid Chocolate, Jimmy McLarnin, Sixto Escobar, Tony Canzoneri, Henry Armstrong, Harry Greb, Sugar Ray Robinson, Rocky Graziano, Rocky Marciano, Bobo Olson, and Archie Moore.

Use of the Polo Grounds wasn't confined to major sporting events; for that matter, it wasn't confined to sporting events at all. The three different Polo Grounds that inhabited Coogan's Hollow hosted almost every type of event—except polo.

Polo, of course, had been a part of the original Polo Grounds on 110th Street and Fifth Avenue in the 1880s. This venue was the site of other attractions, including frequent fireworks exhibitions as well as Buffalo Bill Cody's Wild West Show, which performed a two-week run at the Polo Grounds in June 1884 while the Giants were on a road trip. Cody's shows were held in both the afternoon and evening, with the nighttime performances enhanced by electric and calcium lights that, according to the *New-York Times*, made the grounds as "brilliant as at noonday." Performances weren't allowed on Sunday, so Buffalo Bill instead used the Polo Grounds for a private rib roast on Sunday, June 15.

Other events put people into the original Polo Grounds, both when the Giants were out of town as well as over the off-season. The *New York Sun* reported on a toboggan that had been built in the winter of 1886:

> At the Polo Grounds, 110th street and Fifth avenue, a duplicate of the famous slide at Montreal has been constructed, and tobogganing is to have its "season" with as clear a right to a place among metropolitan amusements as baseball or the opera. The juvenile toboggan rudely began its career in New York in the days of the Dutch, though strangely enough all the historians of the city fail to make mention of the fact.

Another snow-covered hill was also built in a later version of the Polo Grounds as part of the International Winter Sports Carnival in February 1937. Ski jumping as well as downhill and slalom skiing were held on the 225-foot-long slide, which reached 125 feet in the air and towered over the center-field clubhouse.

Musical performances and religious rallies were also a big part of the final Polo Grounds. Grand opera first appeared in 1923 and continued for several summers, working its schedule in between Giants homestands. The Municipal Opera Company of New York opened its 1925 season at the Polo Grounds with Gilbert and Sullivan's *H.M.S. Pinafore*, prompting a headline in the *New York Herald-Tribune*, "Opera Stage to Be Frigate and Polo Grounds a Harbor." The *Herald-Tribune* reported that "the stage will represent an old-fashioned English frigate, moored with one side facing the center of the grandstand so as to afford seats for 15,000 within proper view of the stage. The rest of the field will represent Portsmouth Harbor. The ship is to be 130 feet long and 60 feet wide, built in sections which can be hauled off the grounds between performances."

In October 1943, the Polo Grounds held more than 75,000 people, who listed to Archbishop Francis J. Spellman speak from a large altar that had been erected in center field. Fifteen years later, the American Committee for Israel held a celebration at the Polo Grounds to commemorate the first years of modern Israel's existence. Around this same time, the Watchtower held a one-week rally of Jehovah's Witnesses.

The International Soccer League, in its initial year of operation, played on Sundays at the Polo Grounds in 1960. There was also track and field, tennis, basketball, wrestling, rugby, lacrosse, trapshooting, stock-car racing, midget-car racing, ice skating (with the outfield flooded to provide a rink), and sledge-dog racing at the Polo Grounds at one time or another.

Rodeo was also held there, sometimes with strange results. Ten spectators, including a Peruvian diplomat, were injured when a stunt car skidded into the box seats during a rodeo in July 1942. A few days earlier, one of the rodeo performers—a 1,000-pound fighting bull named Blue Boy—was electrocuted when he escaped while being unloaded and came in contact with a third rail on the elevated tracks at the rear of the Polo Grounds.

Two months after these events, bombs and land mines were exploded in the Polo Grounds outfield, partly demolishing a model village set up by the War Department's Civilian Protection Society to show members of the civilian defense forces what might happen in an enemy air attack.

A haven for everything from football to opera to ethnic festivals, the Polo Grounds was nothing if not functional—and flexible.

APPENDIX A

Polo Grounds Park Factors

BECAUSE OF THEIR NONSTANDARD DIMENSIONS, BASEBALL STADIUMS affect the game, as well as the statistics of teams and individual players, in many different ways. Some ballparks favor a team with power, others a team with speed. Some are friendlier to hitters, while some are graveyards. Distances to the fences at various points, heights of the fences, and other factors such as wind conditions and atmosphere caused by the elevation of the ballpark, all play a part in this phenomenon.

The strange dimensions of the final version of the Polo Grounds, the one rebuilt after the fire in 1911 and lasting until 1963, made it one of the most interesting stadiums in regard to its effect on the game. The question of whether the Polo Grounds favored hitters or pitchers is not an easy one to answer. The response is dependant on the type of hitter or pitcher as well as whether the issue is overall offense or just home runs.

Regarding the stadium's effect on pitchers, John Holway, in his book *The Sluggers*, explains:

> As unkind as the Polo Grounds was to fastball pitchers—the foul lines measured just 258 feet to right, only 250 feet to the upper deck in left, and 279 feet to the lower deck—the monstrous center field, which generally measured 483 feet from home plate, allowed pitchers ample margin for error. Christy Mathewson's fadeaway and Carl Hubbell's screwball enabled these Giants' pitchers to enjoy remarkable success in the big park.

The Polo Grounds could produce the same mixed feelings in hitters. Those who could pull the ball and take advantage of the short distances down the foul lines loved the place; others, whose power was toward the alleys, detested it.

Three of baseball's most prodigious sluggers—Babe Ruth, Mel Ott, and Willie Mays—had the Polo Grounds as their home stadium for at least a few seasons. A breakdown of their statistics at home and on the road helps reveal the influence the Polo Grounds had on their hitting.

Mel Ott

Polo Grounds, 1926–47

	Games	Home Runs	Home Runs/ Plate Appearance	Home Runs/ At Bat	Home Runs/ Game	Batting Average	On-Base Percentage	Slugging Average
Home	1,368	323	.059	.071	.24	.297	.421	.558
Road	1,362	188	.033	.039	.14	.311	.407	.510

Although Ott played more games at home, he had 112 more plate appearances on the road than at home (because the home team will not bat in the last of the ninth if it has already won the game). Even though Ott had a higher batting average on the road, his statistics in the other categories clearly show that the Polo Grounds was well suited to his style of hitting.

Willie Mays

Polo Grounds, 1951–52, 1954–57

	Games	Home Runs	HomeRuns/ Game	Home Runs/ Plate Appearance	Home Runs/ At Bat	Batting Average	On-Base Percentage	Slugging Average
Home	381	94	.25	.059	.066	.319	.319	.592
Road	381	93	.24	.056	.063	.304	.386	.579

Mays had 79 more plate appearances on the road than at home during these years. Even though he was not the type of classic pull hitter who would seem best suited to the Polo Grounds, the configuration of the stadium at least did not detract from his home run total and might have benefited him slightly in his overall hitting.

Babe Ruth

Polo Grounds, 1920–22

	Games	Home Runs	HomeRuns/ Game	Home Runs/ Plate Appearance	Home Runs/ At Bat	Batting Average	On-Base Percentage	Slugging Average
Home	197	75	.38	.090	.115	.379	.505	.849
Road	207	73	.35	.076	.097	.349	.490	.751

Ruth had 124 more plate appearances on the road than at home during the time the Polo Grounds was his home stadium. He left the Polo Grounds following the 1922 season because his team, the Yankees, built its own stadium. Yankee Stadium was presumably designed in such a manner to maximize the effects of Ruth's slugging. However, a look at Ruth's home and road statistics for his first 10 years with Yankee Stadium as his home park shows that his home run totals and overall hitting at home and on the road were close to even. The Polo Grounds, a stadium not designed for Ruth's (or anyone else's) benefit, actually was a friendlier hitting park for him.

Babe Ruth

Yankee Stadium, 1923–32

	Games	Home Runs	Home Runs/ Game	Batting Average	On-Base Percentage	Home Runs/ Slugging Average	Plate Appearance	Home Runs/ At Bat
Home	714	224	.31	.355	.489	.708	.073	.092
Road	704	231	.33	.355	.485	.715	.072	.090

The home versus road statistics illuminate the effect the Polo Grounds had on a few of its most prominent individual tenants. But are they typical? A look at the overall park effects of the Polo Grounds helps to answer that question.

Effects of a particular stadium on home runs can be figured by comparing the total number home runs hit (by both the home and visiting team) against the total hit by both teams in the road games of the team that occupies the stadium in question. For example, in 1946, the Giants and their opponents hit 151 home runs at the Polo Grounds and 84 home runs in Giants games on the road that year (in the same number of games against each opponent). Although other factors may have been present, the discrepancy indicates that the Polo Grounds did contribute greatly to home run production. For the entire history of Polo Grounds IV, from 1911 to 1963, an average of 1.475 home runs were hit per game by both teams; in games involving Polo Grounds occupants played on the road, only .864 home runs per game were hit by both teams, a home to road ratio of 63.1 to 36.9. The former figure is 171 percent of the latter, meaning that home runs were increased by approximately 71 percent because of the characteristics of the ballpark itself.

Another method used to process this information is the comparison of home runs hit per inning by a team at home to home runs hit per inning by the team on the road. These numbers are then refined through a complex formula that takes into account a number of variables and comes up with a figure called a home run factor (although the number will be relatively close to the figure derived from the formula outlined in the previous paragraph).

The home run factor for Giants games in Polo Grounds IV, from 1911 to 1957, was 170 (with 100 being average). How did this compare with other stadiums from the classic era, especially those considered to be conducive to home runs? Wrigley Field in Chicago had a home run factor of 116; Ebbets Field in Brooklyn had a factor of 110; Fenway Park in Boston (after its extensive 1934 remodeling) had a factor of 111; Briggs Stadium (later Tiger Stadium) in Detroit had a factor of 127 after 1938. The only stadium from this period that rivaled the Polo Grounds as a home-run haven was the Baker Bowl in Philadelphia, which had a home run factor of 159. Of all the post-1914 baseball stadiums that were used for more than one year, only one—Coors Field in Denver, which opened in 1995—surpassed the final version of the Polo Grounds in home-run friendliness.

A positive correlation between a stadium's home run factor and its run factor (the effect of a stadium on the total runs scored) often exists, but this isn't always the case, and it certainly wasn't with the Polo Grounds. Even though the Polo Grounds had a home run factor of 170, its run factor was 97, meaning that the stadium's effect was slightly below average in terms of total offense.

The shape of the playing area played a role in this paradox. The Polo Grounds had an extremely spacious outfield, compared with other stadiums, but as John Pastier pointed out, "It was an incredible home-run paradise due to its lilliputian foul lines." The shortness of the foul lines, combined with the deepness to the other reaches of the outfield, made for a narrow field, allowing outfielders to play closer together than they would in other stadiums. As a result, they could cut off more hits before they got through the gaps, turning potential extra-base hits into singles; in addition, the outfielders could corral more fly balls that otherwise might have dropped in, turning potential hits into outs. Also, the large amount of foul territory kept a number of pop flies in play and allowed them to be caught rather than drift safely into the seats and give the batter another chance.

While the short distances down the foul lines created many more home runs at the Polo Grounds, balls that didn't sail over the fences were more likely to become outs there than in other stadiums. Thus, for batted balls that weren't home runs, the Polo Grounds provided an extreme benefit to the pitcher, so much so that it more than offset the stadium's high home run factor.

(As for the earlier versions of the Polo Grounds, the first two were definitely not hitter-friendly, although the third one was, at least in terms of home runs. For the main diamond at Polo Grounds I, used from 1883 to 1888, the run factor was 92 and the home run factor 71. For Polo Grounds II, used in 1889 and 1890, the run factor was 98 and the home run factor 54. For the years that the Giants used Polo Grounds III, from 1891 to the beginning of the 1911 season, the run factor was 97 and the home run factor 134.)

When considering the park factors for Polo Grounds IV, it should be remembered that the park was significantly altered followed the 1922 season. The creation of the overhang in left field that came out of this renovation enhanced home run hitting, although it had a minimal effect on the overall home run factor when compared to the entire history of Polo Grounds IV.

The overhang did make games more interesting for fans, batters, pitchers, and especially outfielders. It also created a situation where it became relatively easy to hit a ball into the upper deck in left field but extremely difficult to tuck one into the lower left-field grandstand.

The historian John McCormack has studied the effect of the overhang in terms of how difficult it became to homer into the lower deck in left field. Of the 204 home runs hit during the regularly scheduled games at the Polo Grounds in 1951 (not counting the two Dodgers-Giants tiebreaker playoff games), he has accounted for the location of 131 of them. "Only one of the 131 went into the lower left-field stands," McCormack said. It was hit by Putsy Caballero of the Phillies and was his only major league home run. As for the others, 33 were hit into the upper deck in right, 80 into the upper deck in left (the upper-deck homers include drives against the facade of the roof or upper deck or off or over the roof), 15 into the lower deck in right, and two inside the park. "For what it's worth," concluded McCormack, "I grew up in New York City between the two world wars. While I saw many games at the Polo Grounds, I didn't see many home runs go into the lower left field stands. Those that did were well hit."

APPENDIX B

Summary of Championship Events and Other Highlights at the Polo Grounds

Championship Boxing Matches

June 2, 1923	Featherweight	Eugene Criqui defeated Johnny Kilbane, 6th-round knockout
June 18, 1923	Flyweight	Pancho Villa defeated Jimmy Wilde, 7th-round knockout
July 26, 1923	Featherweight	Johnny Dundee defeated Eugene Criqui, 15-round decision
August 31, 1923	Middleweight	Harry Greb defeated Johnny Wilson, 15-round decision
September 14, 1923	Heavyweight	Jack Dempsey defeated Luis Firpo, 2nd-round knockout
July 2, 1925	Middleweight	Harry Greb defeated Mickey Walker, 15-round decision
June 3, 1927	Welterweight	Joe Dundee defeated Pete Latzo, 15-round decision
May 21, 1928	Lightweight	Sammy Mandell defeated Jimmy McLarnin, 15-round decision
September 10, 1931	Lightweight	Tony Canzoneri defeated Jack "Kid" Berg, 15-round decision
September 12, 1933	Lightweight	Barney Ross defeated Tony Canzoneri, 15-round decision
May 28, 1935	Welterweight	Barney Ross defeated Jimmy McLarnin, 15-round decision

September 23, 1937	Bantamweight	Harry Jeffra defeated Sixto Escobar, 15-round decision
September 23, 1937	Lightweight	Lou Ambers defeated Pedro Montanez, 15-round decision
September 23, 1937	Welterweight	Barney Ross defeated Ceferino Garcia, 15-round decision
September 23, 1937	Middleweight	Fred Apostoli defeated Marcel Thil, 10th-round technical knockout
June 18, 1941	Heavyweight	Joe Louis defeated Billy Conn, 13th-round knockout
September 29, 1941	Heavyweight	Joe Louis defeated Lou Nova, 6th-round knockout
September 12, 1951	Middleweight	Sugar Ray Robinson defeated Randy Turpin, 10th-round technical knockout
September 26, 1951	Featherweight	Sandy Saddler defeated Willie Pep, 10th-round technical knockout
September 24, 1953	Heavyweight	Rocky Marciano defeated Roland LaStarza, 11th-round technical knockout
June 22, 1955	Light heavy-weight	Archie Moore defeated Carl "Bobo" Olson, 3rd-round knockout
July 29, 1957	Heavyweight	Floyd Patterson defeated Tommy Jackson, 10th-round technical knockout
June 20, 1960	Heavyweight	Floyd Patterson defeated Ingemar Johansson, 5th-round knockout

National Football League Title Games

December 9, 1934

Chicago Bears 13

New York Giants 30

Attendance—35,059

This was the famous "Sneakers Game" in which the Giants, trailing by seven points at halftime, switched from cleated shoes to basketball shoes to improve their footing on the frozen field. New York scored four touchdowns in the fourth quarter, two of them on runs by Ken Strong, one for 42 yards and the other for 11 yards.

December 13, 1936

Green Bay Packers 21
Boston Redskins 6
Attendance—29,545

The game was shifted from Boston to New York because Boston owner George Preston Marshall, in the process of moving the team to Washington, D.C., was disgusted with the poor fan support his team had received in Boston. The Green Bay Packers, playing in their first NFL title game, defeated the Redskins, with quarterback Arnie Herber connecting on touchdown passes with Don Hutson and Milt Gantenbein.

December 11, 1938

Green Bay Packers 17
New York Giants 23
Attendance—48,120

Green Bay held a 17–16 lead in the third quarter when Giants halfback Hank Soar, later an American League umpire, leaped and grabbed a 23-yard pass from Ed Danowski at the goal line, then squirmed into the end zone for the game-winning touchdown. The attendance was a record for a NFL title game.

December 14, 1944

Green Bay Packers 14
New York Giants 7
Attendance—48,120

Green Bay fullback Ted Fritsch ran for one touchdown and caught a pass for another in the second quarter, providing the Packers with all the points they needed for a 14–7 win over the Giants.

December 15, 1946

Chicago Bears 24
New York Giants 14
Attendance—58,346

The crowd of 58,346 broke the attendance record for an NFL title game set at the Polo Grounds eight years earlier, establishing a mark that would last until 1955. Chicago quarterback Sid Luckman had a big game, passing to Ken Kavanaugh for the first touchdown and then breaking a 14–14 tie with a 19-yard bootleg in the fourth quarter. (Three years earlier at the Polo Grounds,

Luckman had set a record by passing for seven touchdowns to lead the Bears to a 56–7 regular-season win over the Giants.)

In addition to the NFL title games, the Polo Grounds hosted an Eastern Division playoff game (needed to break a first-place tie) on December 19, 1943. Before 42,800 spectators, the Washington Redskins beat the Giants, 28–0.

A crowd of 17,725 saw the Pro All Star Game at the Polo Grounds on January 4, 1942. The Chicago Bears, who had won the 1941 NFL championship two weeks before, beat a group of All Stars from the other league teams, 35–24. In the 1950s, the name of the game was changed to the Pro Bowl, and it became a contest between the conferences rather than one involving the championship team against the rest of the league.

Baseball World Series

1884

Providence Grays 3

New York Metropolitans 0

All three games of the best-of-three series were played at the Polo Grounds. Old Hoss Radbourn, who had won 60 games during the regular season, won all three games for Providence. The Grays clinched the series after winning the first two games, but the third game was played anyway. With only a few hundred fans at the Polo Grounds on a cold and windy day, Providence tried to opt out of the final game. They finally agreed to play when New York manager Jim Mutrie offered them the opportunity to select the umpire. The Grays chose Tim Keefe, the Metropolitans' top pitcher. With Keefe umpiring, the Metropolitans had to use rookie Buck Becannon on the mound. Becannon held Providence to three runs over the first four innings, but the Grays exploded for four runs in both the fifth and sixth innings and won the game, which was stopped after six innings, 11–2.

1887

Detroit Wolverines 10

St. Louis Browns 5

The fifth game of this best-of-fifteen World Series was played at the Polo Grounds on October 15 before 3,000 spectators. On a two-hitter by Charlie Getzein, Detroit shut out the Browns, 9–0, to take a four-game-to-one lead in the series. In addition to the Polo Grounds and the home cities of Detroit and St. Louis, games were played in Pittsburgh, Brooklyn, Philadelphia, Boston, Chicago, Baltimore, and Washington (the latter two cities hosting games on the same day).

1888

New York Giants 6
St. Louis Browns 4

The Giants wrapped up the series with six wins in the first eight games, rendering meaningless the Browns' final two wins. Four of the first five games were played at the Polo Grounds. The fifth game, on October 20, was the final game ever at the original Polo Grounds at 110th Street and Fifth Avenue. Tim Keefe was the winning pitcher in that game as the Giants came up with five runs in the last of the eighth inning for a 6–4 victory.

1889

New York Giants 6
Brooklyn Bridegrooms 3

This was the only World Series played in Polo Grounds II. After falling behind, three games to one, the Giants won the final five games of the series. Hank O'Day was the winning pitcher in two of those victories. Nineteen years later, O'Day was the umpire who ruled Fred Merkle out for not touching second base in a key game between the Giants and Cubs during the 1908 pennant race.

1894 (Temple Cup)

New York Giants 4
Baltimore Orioles 0

This was the first year of the Temple Cup Series, held between the top two finishers in the National League. The Giants finished second to the Baltimore Orioles during the regular season but swept the Orioles in the series.

1905

New York Giants 4
Philadelphia Athletics 1

All five of the games were shutouts, with three of them hurled by Christy Mathewson. The second, fourth, and fifth games were at the Polo Grounds. In the second game, Chief Bender of Philadelphia shut out the Giants on four hits. In Game 4, Joe "Iron Man" McGinnity outdueled Eddie Plank of Philadelphia, giving the Giants a 1–0 win and a three-game-to-one lead in the series. The next day Mathewson finished it off with a 2–0 win over Bender and the Athletics, Mathewson's third shutout in six days.

1911

Philadelphia Athletics 4
New York Giants 2

This was the series that christened Frank Baker of the Athletics as "Home Run" Baker. Baker—the third baseman in Philadelphia's $100,000 infield (which also had shortstop Jack Barry, second baseman Eddie Collins, and first baseman Stuffy McInnis)—had led the American League with nine home runs in 1911. Still, his prowess with the long ball didn't earn him his nickname until the 1911 World Series. In the second game, at Philadelphia, Baker broke a 1–1 tie in the sixth inning with a two-run homer off Rube Marquard. The next day, at the Polo Grounds, he connected in the ninth inning off Mathewson to send the game into extra innings. The Athletics won the game in 11 innings and went on to win the series.

The Giants, after having stolen a record 347 bases during the regular season, could manage only 4 steals in the six-game series.

1912

Boston Red Sox 4
New York Giants 3
1 tie game

The highlights of this series came in Boston's Fenway Park. In the third game, the Giants held a 2–1 lead in the last of the ninth, but Boston had runners on second and third with two out when Forrest Cady hit a long fly to right-center field. In the dusk and fog that had settled over the playing area, Josh Devore of the Giants made a tremendous running catch and, without breaking stride, continued on to the clubhouse, leaving much of the crowd in a state of confusion. Many left the game celebrating a Red Sox victory, some not realizing until they read the newspaper that Devore had made the catch to preserve a New York victory.

The ending to the final game of the series was nearly as bizarre. New York had taken a 2–1 lead in the top of the tenth inning. Facing Christy Mathewson, Clyde Engle opened the last of the tenth with a fly to center that Fred Snodgrass dropped. Snodgrass redeemed himself with a great running catch of a drive hit by the next batter, Harry Hooper, but then first baseman Fred Merkle got into the act. After Steve Yerkes walked, Merkle let a pop fly by Tris Speaker fall safely in foul territory. Given another chance, Speaker singled to score Engle with the tying run and send Yerkes to third. Yerkes then came home on a sacrifice fly to win the game and the series for Boston.

1913

Philadelphia Athletics 4
New York Giants 1

Christy Mathewson's 10-inning shutout in Game 2 was the only win for the Giants in the series. Mathewson beat Eddie Plank, but three days later, Plank came out on top of a duel with Mathewson at the Polo Grounds, winning, 3–1, to wrap up the series for Philadelphia.

1917

Chicago White Sox 4
New York Giants 2

A strange play at the Polo Grounds was the focal point of the final game. With the game scoreless in the top of the fourth inning, Chicago had Eddie Collins on third base and Joe Jackson on first when Happy Felsch hit a grounder back to Giants pitcher Rube Benton. Collins had broken for the plate when Felsch hit the ball and appeared to be trapped as Benton threw to third baseman Heinie Zimmerman, who began running Collins down. Collins was able to dart past catcher Bill Rariden, who had come up the line to take Zimmerman's throw and then found home plate uncovered. With no one to throw to, Zimmerman ran after the runner but was no match for the fleet Collins and looked foolish in the attempt. The play was the beginning of a three-run rally for Chicago, which went on to a 4–2 win and the championship. Zimmerman was seen as the goat on the play for his futile chase of Collins, although the blame really lay with Benton and first baseman Walter Holke for their failure to back up Rariden and cover the plate.

Urban "Red" Faber won three games without a loss in the series for the White Sox.

1921

New York Giants 5
New York Yankees 3

This was the first twentieth-century World Series in which all the games were played in one stadium, the first championship meeting between the Giants and Yankees, and the last series played with a best-of-nine format. The Yankees won the first two games—both by scores of 3–0 on a seven-hitter by Carl Mays in the opener and a two-hitter by Waite Hoyt in the second game—but the Giants won five of the final six to take the series. Shufflin' Phil Douglas, the loser in Game 1, beat Mays in the fourth and seventh games. In the eighth and final game, Art Nehf—who had already lost twice to Hoyt in the series—came out on top, holding the Yankees to four hits in outdueling Hoyt and winning, 1–0.

1922

New York Giants 4
New York Yankees 0
1 tie game

The most notable game in this series was the one that wasn't played to a decision. In the second game, the Giants took the lead in the top of the first on a three-run homer by Irish Meusel, but the Yankees battled back with single runs in the first, fourth, and eighth innings. The game was still tied, 3–3, after 10 innings, when plate umpire George Hildebrand called the game on account of darkness, even though there appeared to be enough daylight left for at least two more innings. Commissioner Kenesaw Mountain Landis, confronted by an angry mob of fans who thought he was responsible for the decision, later announced that the gate receipts from the game would be donated to military hospitals for disabled veterans.

In the series—the second straight in which all the games were played at the Polo Grounds—Giants pitchers held Babe Ruth to a single and a double in 17 at bats.

1923

New York Yankees 4
New York Giants 2

The Yankees finally had a stadium of their own, but it didn't help them initially, as their only two losses in the series came in the first two games at Yankee Stadium. The Giants won both of those games on home runs by Casey Stengel. Stengel hit an inside-the-park homer in the ninth inning to give the Giants a 5–4 win; he then homered in the seventh inning of Game 3 as the Giants won, 1–0.

The Yankees, however, won the other game played at Yankee Stadium, as well as all three played at the Polo Grounds, to win their first world championship.

1924

Washington Senators 4
New York Giants 3

In the series for the fourth straight year, the Giants faced Walter Johnson and the Washington Senators, playing in their first world championship. The

Giants took a three-game-to-two lead with a 6–2 win at the Polo Grounds in Game 5. Jack Bentley, in addition to being the winning pitcher in the game, hit a two-run homer off Walter Johnson into the upper deck in right field.

Back in Washington, the Senators won the sixth and seventh games—the final one in 12 innings—to win the World Series.

1933

New York Giants 4

Washington Senators 1

The Giants won the first two games, at the Polo Grounds, then took two out of three in Washington to win the series. In the first game, Carl Hubbell struck out 10 batters, and Mel Ott had four hits in a 4–2 win. The Giants won again the next day, 6–1, behind the pitching of "Prince Hal" Schumacher.

1936

New York Yankees 4

New York Giants 2

Behind Carl Hubbell, the Giants won Game 1, at the Polo Grounds, but were trounced the next day, 18–4, in front of a Polo Grounds crowd that included President Franklin Roosevelt. This game ended with Yankees center fielder Joe DiMaggio corralling a long drive by Hank Leiber and then starting up the clubhouse steps, only to come to an abrupt halt when he remembered that the crowd had been requested to remain until the president had departed. "Modest Joe considered himself one of the crowd and decided not to move," reported the *New York Times* the next day. "He was almost knocked down a couple of times by the returning automobiles [of the presidential entourage] and finally was induced to join the other players in the exodus to the clubhouse." (Roosevelt had planned on leaving midway through the game, but he was so enthralled by the action that he stayed until the end, even though it made him late for his scheduled appearance at the groundbreaking of the Queens-Midtown Tunnel under the East River.) The Yankees won three of the next four games, including another rout at the Polo Grounds, a 13–5 game in the sixth and final game of the series.

1937

New York Yankees 4

New York Giants 1

The Giants only win in this series came at the Polo Grounds, after the Yankees had won the first three games. Carl Hubbell was on the mound for the

Giants for their sole win, but the Yankees won the next day to become the first team to win six World Series.

1946

Newark Eagles 4
Kansas City Monarchs 3

The first game of this series for the Negro Leagues championship was played at the Polo Grounds on Tuesday, September 17, with the Monarchs defeating the Eagles, 2–1. Satchel Paige, in relief, was the winning pitcher and also scored the winning run in the seventh inning. Newark went on to win the series, however, with the other games played in Kansas City and Newark as well as at Comiskey Park in Chicago.

1947

New York Cubans 4
Cleveland Buckeyes 1
1 tie game

The Cubans, champions of the Negro National League, opened the series against the Buckeyes on Friday, September 19, at the Polo Grounds. Luis Tiant, Sr., the Cubans' 42-year-old southpaw who was unbeaten that season, was scheduled to start for New York; however, Dave Barnhill was instead on the mound for the Cubans, facing Chet Brewer of the Buckeyes. Rain interfered with the game, in addition to holding the attendance down to about 4,000 (well below the projected 20,000), and caused it to end as a 5–5 tie after six innings.

Barnhill was knocked out in the second inning on a three-run homer by Johnny Cowan that put Cleveland ahead, 5–0. The Cubans came back with single runs in the second and fourth, then tied the game with three runs in the fifth on three singles, a walk, and a double by Lorenzo Cabrera. Cleveland scored in the seventh, but the run was nullified when the game was rained out before the entire inning could be completed. It was the only game of the series played at the Polo Grounds.

The Cleveland roster included Sad Sam Jones and Sam Jethro. The Cubans—who eventually won the series, four games to one—had Minnie Minoso, Ray Noble, and Pat Scantlebury.

1951

New York Yankees 4
New York Giants 2

The Giants took a two-game-to-one lead in the series but lost the next three games—two of them at the Polo Grounds—to the Yankees. The series started after a draining three-game pennant playoff between the Giants and Brooklyn Dodgers. The Giants had won the playoff opener, 3–1, at Ebbets Field, then dropped the second game, 10–0, at the Polo Grounds. The third game, also at the Polo Grounds, was won by the Giants, 5–4, on a three-run homer by Bobby Thomson with one out in the last of the ninth.

1954

New York Giants 4
Cleveland Indians 0

The Giants won the first game on Willie Mays's great catch in the eighth inning to preserve a 2–2 and on Dusty Rhodes's three-run homer that broke the tie in the tenth inning. Rhodes had a run-scoring single and another home run the next day as the Giants won, 3–1, in the final World Series game ever played at the Polo Grounds. The Giants completed the series sweep with wins in the next two games, at Cleveland.

Multiteam Doubleheaders

In the 1880s and 1890s, the Polo Grounds was the scene of several doubleheaders involving several teams and, in some cases, more than one league. The issue of multiteam, multileague doubleheaders became a hot topic again in April 1998, after an expansion joint fell from the underside of the upper deck in Yankee Stadium, causing the Yankees to resort to different methods while the structural integrity of their home was evaluated. One of their games was moved to Shea Stadium in Queens, home of the Mets, where, on April 15, 1998, the Yankees played an afternoon game against the Anaheim Angels, and the Mets followed with a game against the Chicago Cubs that night.

Although historians have been unable to find another example of this type of a doubleheader—with an American League game and a National League game being played in the same stadium in the same day—there have been other examples of doubleheaders involving more than two teams and/or more than one league, with several of them taking place in the Polo Grounds.

Two games involving four teams from three leagues occurred at the Polo Grounds on Tuesday, September 17, 1946. The New York Giants and St. Louis Cardinals played in the afternoon. At night the Polo Grounds then hosted the opening game of the Negro World Series between the Newark Eagles of the Negro National League and the Kansas City Monarchs of the Negro American League. (Another same-stadium doubleheader involving the National League and a Negro league took place at Forbes Field in Pittsburgh on Saturday, May 7, 1932, when the game between the Pittsburgh Pirates and Philadelphia Phillies was followed by a Negro East-West League game between the Homestead Grays and Cleveland Stars.)

Doubleheaders involving multiple teams were even more common in the nineteenth century. The Metropolitans of the American Association played against two teams on Decoration Day in both 1883 and 1884. The 1883 doubleheader, on the west diamond of the original Polo Grounds, had the Metropolitans playing Cincinnati in the morning and Columbus in the afternoon. In 1884 the split-doubleheader took place at Metropolitan Park and was held in conjunction with a similar doubleheader in Brooklyn. In the forenoon, the Metropolitans beat St. Louis at Metropolitan Park while Brooklyn was shutting out Indianapolis at Washington Park in Brooklyn. St. Louis and Indianapolis then crossed paths with Indianapolis, playing, and beating, the Metropolitans at Metropolitan Park in the afternoon as St. Louis was defeating Brooklyn at Washington Park. (In addition to these doubleheaders, in the 1890s the Chicago National League team was known to have played doubleheaders against different opponents on various occasions; the New York National League team did so at least once in the 1880s—on Independence Day in 1883, when the New-Yorks beat Boston in the morning and Providence in the afternoon. Another example of this type of doubleheader occurred at Robison Field in St. Louis in September of 1899, when the Louisville Colonels played National League games against the St. Louis Cardinals and Cleveland Spiders on the same day.)

As for doubleheaders involving teams from different leagues on the same field on the same day, this happened at the Polo Grounds on several occasions late in the 1885 season. The first time such a doubleheader was scheduled was Tuesday, August 25, 1885, but rain postponed the event. The following afternoon the Metropolitans hosted Baltimore at 2:00, with the New-Yorks playing Providence immediately after. The *New-York Times* report of the August 26 games said: "The day was raw and chilly and anything but pleasant for the spectators. In spite of this drawback, over 3,000 persons sat four hours and witnessed both games. They managed to keep their blood in circulation by vigorously stamping with their feet at every good play."

Here are the dates and results of the two-league doubleheaders on the Polo Grounds in 1885:

Wednesday, August 26

American Association—Metropolitans 8, Baltimore 2
National League—New York 6, Providence 0

Friday, August 28

American Association—Athletic Club of Philadelphia 4, Metropolitans 2
National League—New York 3, Boston 1

Thursday, September 10

American Association—Metropolitans 4, Louisville 2
National League—New York 8, Providence 1 (6 innings, called by darkness)

Wednesday, September 23

American Association—St. Louis 7, Metropolitans 4
National League—New York 17, Buffalo 2

Thursday, September 24

American Association—Metropolitans 5, Cincinnati 2
National League—New York 11, Buffalo 3 (7 innings, called by darkness)

Saturday, September 26

American Association—Metropolitans 7, Cincinnati 2
National League—New York 4, Buffalo 1

In addition to these games, both the Metropolitans and the New-Yorks played on the Polo Grounds on Saturday, September 12, although the National League game between New York and Providence was only an exhibition game.

(The Giants and the Polo Grounds were involved in a different type of doubleheader on Labor Day 1903. New York and Brooklyn met in a pair of games at separate parks. The morning game was played at Washington Park in Brooklyn and won by the Giants, 6–4. The teams, followed by many of their fans, then crossed the East River and headed uptown for the afternoon game, which was played at the Polo Grounds. Brooklyn prevailed in this game, 3–0. Although two-site doubleheaders were sometimes a regular occurence in the minors, it was nearly 97 years before such a doubleheader was played again in the major leagues.)

Memorial Plaques

Following is the list of men who were honored with plaques in center field at the Polo Grounds, along with the dates that the plaques were unveiled:

Edward L. Grant—May 30, 1921
Christy Mathewson—September 27, 1928
Ross Youngs—September 27, 1928
John McGraw—July 10, 1934
Al Blozis—December 2, 1945
Jack Lummus—December 2, 1945
James J. Walker—July 11, 1948

Eddie Grant's tablet was on a freestanding monument in front of the clubhouse wall; the remainder were on the wall. John McGraw's was in the middle and above the others, which, from left to right, were Jack Lummus, Christy Mathewson, Jimmy Walker, Ross Youngs, and Al Blozis.

Some mystery surrounds the fate of these plaques. Photographs indicate that all were present when the New York Giants played their final game at the Polo Grounds on September 29, 1957. Photos also show that the plaques were no longer in place when the New York Mets began playing in the Polo Grounds in 1962 (although the monument that had once held the Grant tablet was still there).

Newspaper accounts of the New York Giants' final game in 1957 report the pillaging of the Polo Grounds following the game and indicate that the Grant tablet, although torn loose from the monument by souvenir hunters, was recovered by the police. What happened after that is unclear. Everett Parker, who spent nearly 33 years with the New York Police Department (NYPD), wondered if the Eddie Grant tablet would have been turned in, even if it had been recovered. "The correct procedure on stolen or lost property was to take it to the precinct in which the property was recovered," Parker explained:

> However, herein lies another NYPD fact of life. No cop would approach a Lieutenant Desk officer with something like this. Harlem, the home of the 32nd precinct [in which the Polo Grounds was located], at this time was the busiest in NYC. Desk officers using 600-page blotters wrote everything by hand that transpired during their tour. . . . The "boss" faced with cops returning a tablet for vouchering would have told them to "get lost."

Parker was able to track down the blotters used on September 29, 1957, the date of the final game of the New York Giants, but they showed nothing about tablets being vouchered on that day (nor on the ensuing days). "If the cops confiscated it," Parker concluded, "that tablet went into someone's den."

One plaque did turn up decades after it disappeared. In 1999, Stuart Leeds, the president of the New York (baseball) Giants Historical Society, stopped to look at a display of New York baseball memorabilia in the window of a J. Peterman Store in midtown Manhattan. Amid the relics was a large gray-green object that caught Leeds's eye. Upon closer inspection, he discovered that it was the plaque for Jack Lummus. Leeds contacted the New York Giants football team, who purchased the Lummus plaque for $4,000. It is now on display in the football team's offices at Giants Stadium.

The whereabouts of the other plaques remain a mystery.

Essay on Sources

BASIC STATISTICAL INFORMATION ON TEAMS AND PLAYERS COMES PRImarily from *The Baseball Encyclopedia*, Fourth Edition, ed. Joseph Reichler (New York: Macmillan Publishing Company, 1979).

The predominant source for particular details on individual seasons and games are newspapers of the time. Newspapers used in this research include the *Boston Globe*, *Chicago Tribune*, *Los Angeles Times*, *New York Clipper*, *New York Daily Mirror*, *New York Herald*, *New York Herald Tribune*, *New York Sun*, *New-York Times* (the *Times* dropped the hyphen in "New York" on December 1, 1896, *New-York Tribune* (the *Tribune* dropped the hyphen in "New York" on April 16, 1914), *The World*, New York (the *New York World* until May 11, 1883), *New York World-Telegram and Sun*, *Philadelphia Public Ledger*, and *Pittsburgh Courier*.

Maps and atlases from the New York Public Library and the Library of Congress proved helpful.

Chapter 1—Oddest of the Odd

Page

3 Foul line distances: Philip J. Lowry, *Green Cathedrals* (Cooperstown, NY: Society for American Baseball Research [SABR], 1986), pp. 64–65.

3 Ownership of Coogan's Bluff: Jerry Lansche, *Glory Fades Away* (Dallas: Taylor Publishing, 1991), p. 158; Lowell Reidenbaugh, *Take Me Out to the Ball Park* (St. Louis: The Sporting News, 1983), p. 166; Joseph Durso, *The Days of Mr. McGraw* (Englewood Cliffs, NJ: 1969), p. 43; Kenneth T. Jackson, ed., *The Encyclopedia of New York City* (New Haven and Lon-

don: Yale University Press and The New-York Historical Society, 1995), p. 279; "Who Owns the Grounds?" *New-York Times,* Tuesday, June 25, 1889, p. 2.

3 Recent history of region of Coogan's Bluff: Norval White, *New York: A Physical History* (New York: Atheneum, 1987), p. xxvi; John Hogrogian, "The Polo Grounds Case: Part II," *The Coffin Corner*, vol. 12, no. 6 (1990), p. 4; John Thorn and Pete Palmer, eds., *Total Baseball*, Fourth Edition (New York: Viking, 1995), p. 96; Donald A. Mackay, *The Building of Manhattan* (New York: Harper & Row, 1987); "First Map Extended Manhattan Streets Eight Miles into Farmlands," *New York Times*, Monday, March 20, 1961, p. 31.

3–4 Public transit: Brian J. Cudahy, *Under the Sidewalks of New York*, Revised Edition (Lexington, MA: The Stephen Greene Press, 1988), p. 12; Susan E. Lyman, *The Face of New York: The City as It Was and as It Is* (New York: Crown Publishers, Inc., 1954); Jackson, ed., *The Encyclopedia of New York City*, pp. 368–369; Eric Homberger, *The Historical Atlas of New York* (New York: Henry Holt and Company, Inc., 1994), pp. 106–107.

4 Creamer quote: Robert Creamer, "The Quaint Cult of the Mets," *Sports Illustrated*, May 6, 1963, p. 61.

4 Stein response: Fred Stein, *Under Coogan's Bluff* (n.p.: 1978), p. 3.

4 Hawkins's memories: Interview with Dr. Seth C. Hawkins, December 19, 1997.

5 Curtis quote: Paul Dickson, *Baseball's Greatest Quotations* (New York: HarperCollins Publishers, 1991), p. 98.

5 Garreau quote: Garth Garreau, *Bat Boy of the Giants* (Philadelphia: The Westminster Press, 1948), p. 12.

5 Schwab quote: Interview with Jerry Schwab, December 14, 1997.

5 Park factors: John Thorn and Pete Palmer, eds., *Total Baseball* (New York: Warner Books, 1989), pp. 2169–2170; correspondence with John Pastier, 1997–98; research of Kevin Cluff.

6 1948 game: "Giants Defeat Dodgers on Conway's Wind-Blown Home Run in Ninth" by Louis Effrat, *New York Times*, Monday, July 12, 1948, p. 13.

6 Stein quote: Stein, *Under Coogan's Bluff*, p. 3.

Chapter 2—The Original Polo Grounds

Page

7 Union Grounds: Lowry, *Green Cathedrals*, p. 39; Frederick Ivor-Campbell, ed., *Baseball's First Stars* (Cleveland: Society for American Baseball Research, 1996), p. 21.

8 Bennett: Steven D. Price and Charles Kauffman, *The Polo Primer* (Lexington, Mass.: S. Greene Press, 1989), pp. 2,4; Jackson, ed., *The Encyclopedia of New York City*, p. 101; "Polo Grounds Named Through Gordon Bennett," *New York Sun*, Friday, January 23, 1931; "A Federal Writers' Project," *New York City Guide* (New York: Random House, 1939), p. 256.

8 Day: Noel Hynd, *The Giants of the Polo Grounds* (New York: Doubleday, 1988), pp. 22–23; Ivor-Campbell, ed., *Baseball's First Stars*, p. 49 (biographical entry by David Pietrusza); "John B. Day's Funeral Held" by Will Wedge, *New York Sun*, Wednesday, January 28, 1925.

9 Mutrie: Robert L. Tiemann and Mark Rucker, eds., *Nineteenth-Century Stars* (Cooperstown, NY: Society for American Baseball Research, 1989), p. 98 (biographical entry by John J. O'Malley).

9–10 1880 New York area teams: Lansche, *Glory Fades Away;* James D. Hardy, Jr., *The New York Giants Base Ball Club: The Growth of a Team and a Sport* (Jefferson, NC: McFarland & Company, Inc., 1996), pp. 45–46; William N. Rankin, "Marvelous Growth of Baseball in New York City from Its Humble Origin," c. 1905 (city and publisher unknown); Michael Gershman, *Diamonds* (Boston: Houghton Mifflin Company, 1993), p. 40; "Badly-Beaten at Base-Ball," *New-York Times*, Thursday, September 16, 1880, p. 2; "Base-Ball: The Advent of the Metropolitans," *New York World*, September 16, 1880, p. 2.

9 Proposal to fill East River: "Happy 100th Birthday, New York!" CNN Interactive (http://www.cnn.com/US/9712/28/ny.bday/), December 28, 1997.

10 First game on Polo Grounds: Rankin, "Marvelous Growth of Baseball in New York City"; "Base-Ball on the Polo Grounds," *New-York World*, Thursday, September 30, 1880, p. 8; "Metropolitan Base-Ball: The Opening Match at the Polo Grounds," *New York World*, September 30, 1880, p. 2. (*The World* lists the final score as 4–2, the *Times* as 8–3.)

10 Low attendance at Troy and Worcester: "Chicagos 10, Troys 8," *Boston Globe*, Wednesday, September 28, 1881, p. S1; "The Troys Find the Worcesters an Easy Prey," *Boston Globe*, Saturday, September 30, 1882, p. 1.

11 New York teams joining American Association and National League: David Nemec, *The Beer and Whisky League* (New York: Lyons & Burford, 1994), p. 21; Hardy, *The New York Giants Base Ball Club*, pp. 31–37; David Nemec, *The Great Encyclopedia of 19th-Century Major League Baseball* (New York: Donald I. Fine Books, 1997), p. 39.

Chapter 3—Major League Baseball in New York

Page

13–14 Differences in how game was played: Bill James, *The Bill James Historical Baseball Abstract* (New York: Villard Books, 1985), pp. 22–24; interview with Bob Tholkes, nineteenth-century baseball expert, March 1998; Thorn and Palmer, eds., *Total Baseball* (1989), pp. 2222–2226; Nemec, *The Beer and Whisky League*, p. 14; Nemec, *The Great Encyclopedia of 19th-Century Major League Baseball*, p. 217.

15 First National League game on Polo Grounds: "Opening with a Victory: A Great Crowd to See New York Beat the Boston Nine to Start With," *New York Sun*, Wednesday, May 2, 1883; "Baseball News," *New-York Tribune*, May 2, 1883, p. 2; "Base-Ball: New York Beats Boston in the First League Game Played in this City," *New York World*, May 2, 1883, p. 8; "A Fine Game at the Bat: The New York and Boston Clubs Compete," *New-York Times*, May 2, 1883, p. 2; "Base Ball: The League Season Inaugurated," *Boston Globe*, May 2, 1883, p. 4.

16 First home run on Polo Grounds: David W. Vincent, ed., *Home Runs in the Old Ballparks* (Cleveland: Society for American Baseball Research, 1995), p. 31; "Baseball News," *New-York Tribune*, Thursday, May 3, 1883, p. 2; "The New-Yorks Win Again," *New-York Times*, May 3, 1883, p. 3.

16–19 Different diamonds on Polo Grounds: Philip J. Lowry, *Green Cathedrals*, rev. ed. (Reading, MA: Addison-Wesley Publishing Company, Inc., 1992), pp. 188–189; research of Bob Tiemann; Nemec, *The Great Encyclopedia of 19th-Century Major League Baseball*, p. 209; "Baseball," *New York Clipper*, Saturday, January 6, 1883, p. 674; "The Metropolitan Club," *New York Clipper*, Saturday, January 13, 1883, p. 695; "The Conference Meeting," *New York Clipper*, Saturday, February 17, 1883, p. 775; "Starry Sparks from the Diamond, *New York Clipper*, Saturday, March 17, 1883, p. 840; "The Ball Field," *The World*, Saturday, May 12, 1883, p. 8; "Base-Ball Notes," *The World*, Wednesday, May 30, 1883; "Five Games of Base-

Ball at the Polo Grounds," *New-York Times*, Thursday, May 31, 1883, p. 2; "Other Polo Ground Games," *The World*, May 31, 1883, p. 3; "Baseball News," *New-York Tribune*, Friday, June 1, 1883, p. 5; "Baseball," *New York Clipper*, Saturday, June 9, 1883, p. 188; "The Ball Field," *The World*, September 5, 1883, p. 2.

17 Amputee game: "Sports Today," *New York Times*, Friday, September 12, 1947, p. 27.

17 Sullivan: "Sullivan Playing Base-Ball," *New-York Times*, Tuesday, May 29, 1883, p. 2; "Sullivan Wields the Bat," *New York Sun*, May 29, 1883; "Baseball News," *New-York Tribune*, May 29, 1883, p. 2; "Sullivan to the Bat," *The World*, May 29, 1883, p. 2.

18 Portable fence: Lowry, *Green Cathedrals* (Addison-Wesley), pp. 188–189; "Both Local Nines Beaten," *New-York Times*, Friday, August 31, 1883, p. 3; "Baseball News," *New-York Tribune*, August 31, 1883, p. 2; "Boston vs. New York," *New York Clipper*, Saturday, September 8, 1883, p. 403.

19–21 Metropolitan Park: Lynch quote, Nemec, *The Beer and Whisky League*, p. 61; Lowry, *Green Cathedrals* (SABR), p. 63; John J. O'Malley, "Mutrie's Mets of 1884," *The National Pastime*, Spring 1985, pp. 39–41; "The American Association Meeting," *New York Clipper*, Saturday, September 8, 1883, p. 401; "Baseball," *New York Clipper*, Saturday, December 15, 1883, p. 647; "Baseball," *New York Clipper*, Saturday, January 19, 1884, p. 745; "Baseball," *New York Clipper*, Saturday, February 2, 1884, p. 783; "Base-Ball Games," *New-York Times*, Wednesday, May 14, 1884, p. 2; "Home Nines Victorious: The Allegheny Club Meets Defeat on the New Grounds," *The World*, May 14, 1884.

21 Providence Grays/1884 "World's Series": Jerry Lansche, *The Forgotten Championships* (Jefferson, NC: McFarland & Company, Inc., 1989), pp. 6–9; Nemec, *The Beer and Whisky League*, p. 69.

21–22 Consolidation of best players: Nemec, *The Beer and Whisky League*, p. 91; "Baseball Games," *New-York Times*, Saturday, April 11, 1885, p. 2 (source of Day's quote).

23 Nickname: "Day, First Owner of Giants, Dies," *New York Times*, Monday, January 26, 1925, p. 12; Hynd, *The Giants of the Polo Grounds*, p. 39; references to the "New York Giants" first seen in the *New-York Times* in August 1885.

23 Engel recollections: "Giants' First Batboy Is Not Entirely Alone" by Howard M. Tuckner, *New York Times*, Sunday, September 29, 1957, p. S3.

23–24 Giants fans: "On the Diamond Field," *New-York Times*, Thursday, July 23, 1885, p. 2; "Old Giant Rooter Hushed by Death: 'Well, Well, Well!' Wood Was One [sic] Barred from Field for Shrieks" by Heywood Broun, *New York Tribune*, Friday, December 11, 1914, p. 10; Zane Grey, "Old Well-Well," *The Redheaded Outfield and Other Baseball Stories* (New York: Grosset & Dunlap Publishers, 1920), pp. 223–238.

24 Wiman: Lowry, *Green Cathedrals* (SABR), p. 63; Hynd, *The Giants of the Polo Grounds*, p. 38; Nemec, *The Beer and Whisky League*, p. 114.

24–25 Record crowd: "Winning Even Honors," *New-York Times*, Tuesday, June 1, 1886, p. 2.

25 Sunday baseball ban: "On the Diamond Field" and "Sunday Ball Playing in Ohio," *New-York Times*, Tuesday, May 5, 1885, p. 2; David W. Zang, *Fleet Walker's Divided Heart: The Life of Baseball's First Black Major Leaguer* (Lincoln: University of Nebraska Press, 1995), pp. 50–51.

25–26 Mascots: "The St. Louis Men Beaten," *New-York Times*, Sunday, July 19, 1885, p. 5; "Baseball News," *New-York Times*, Monday, August 3, 1885, p. 5; "Giants Beat Themselves," *New-York Tribune*, Friday, August 30, 1889, p. 3.

26 Home run factor: Thorn and Palmer, eds., *Total Baseball, Fourth Edition* (1995), p. 2237;

Connor: Ivor-Campbell, ed., *Baseball's First Stars*, pp. 38–39 (biographical entry by Bernard J. Crowley); "They Were Only Homesick: New-York Boys Play Ball on the Polo Grounds and Give the Bean-Eaters a Good Drubbing—Connor Makes a Wonderful Hit," *New-York Times*, Sunday, September 12, 1886, p. 5; "At Last New-York Wins a Game," *New-York Tribune*, September 12, 1886, p. 8.

26–27 29–1 game: "The Work of the Giants: They Give the Quaker City Aggregation a Terrible Drubbing," *The World*, Thursday, June 16, 1887, p. 6; "The Giants Get Revenge," *New-York Times*, June 16, 1887, p. 2.

27 Eviction from Polo Grounds: Hardy, *The New York Giants Base Ball Club*, pp. 84–88; Hynd, *The Giants of the Polo Grounds*, p. 60; Michael Benson, *Ballparks of North America* (Jefferson, NC: McFarland & Company, Inc.), p. 255; Henry Moscow, *The Street Book: An Encyclopedia of Manhattan's Street Names and Their Origins* (New York: Hagstrom Company, Inc., 1978), p. 52.

Chapter 4—New Location, Same Name

Page

41 St. George Cricket Grounds: Hardy, *The New York Giants Base Ball Club*, pp. 85–86; Lowry, *Green Cathedrals* (SABR), p. 63.

41–42 New site for stadium: "A New Baseball Field: The Giants Will Play Games in This City Again: Grounds Secured on the West Side of Town in a Convenient Place," *New-York Times*, Saturday, June 22, 1889, p. 2; "The Giants New Grounds: A Home for Them on Manhattan Island at Last," *New-York Tribune*, June 22, 1889, p. 7; "An Adverse Claim at the New Polo Grounds," *New-York Tribune*, Tuesday, June 25, 1889, p. 3.

42–43 Bridges over Harlem River: I. N. Phelps Stokes, *The Iconography of Manhattan Island, 1498-1909* (New York: Robert H. Dodd, 1926); "A Federal Writers' Project," *New York City Guide*, p. 518.

43 First game at New Polo Grounds: "The Giants Are at Home: They Open Their New Grounds in Grand Style," *New-York Times*, Tuesday, July 9, 1889, p. 3; "A Royal Christening: Happy Giants Welcomed to Their New Grounds," *New-York Tribune*, July 9, 1889, p. 2.

44 Panic in grandstand: "Giants Beat Themselves: Two Panics at the New Polo Grounds," *New-York Tribune*, Friday, August 30, 1889, p. 3; "One Victory for Boston," *New-York Times*, August 30, 1889, p. 3; "Batting Holes in the Air," *New-York Tribune*, Saturday, August 31, 1889, p. 3.

44 Anson/Gore: "A Rousing Good-By: Giants Take the Last Two Games on the Home Grounds," *New-York Tribune*, Sunday, September 15, 1889.

45 Rivalry with Brooklyn: "One Game for Brooklyn," *New-York Times*, Saturday, October 19, 1889, p. 3.

45 1889 World Series versus Brooklyn: Mutrie quote, "Giants Beaten by a Run," *New-York Times*, Wednesday, October 23, 1889, p. 3; Ewing quote, "The Brooklyns Win Again," *New-York Times*, Thursday, October 24, 1889, p. 3.

46 Coogan: "Baseballists Up in Arms: A League Composed of Brotherhood Players May Now Be Formed," *The World*, Saturday, September 21, 1889, p. 2.

47 Opening of 1890 Season: "The Season of Baseball," *New-York Times*, Sunday, April 20, 1890, p. 3

47 Brotherhood War/Tiernan home run: Allan Sangree, "No More War in Baseball: Great Conflicts in the History of the Game, Part I," *Baseball Magazine*, August 1911, p. 26; "Victory in 13 Innings: New York Wins from Boston in Thirteen Innings," *The World*, Tuesday, May 13, 1890, p. 6; "Tiernan's Home Run Won It," *New-York Times*, May 13, 1890, p. 3.

48 Gladiators' use of Polo Grounds: Nemec, *The Beer and Whisky League*, p. 192; Lowry, *Green Cathedrals* (SABR), p. 63.

Chapter 5—Polo Grounds III

Page

49–50 Grandstand protruding into foul territory: Lowry, *Green Cathedrals* (Addison-Wesley), p. 191; *Leslie's Illustrated Weekly*, May 7, 1903, pp. 468–469.

50 First game at Polo Grounds III: "To Open the Baseball Season: Elaborate Arrangements for the League's First Schedule Game," *New-York Daily Tribune*, Wednesday, April 22, 1891, p. 5; "The Ball Is Set Rolling: Giants Lose Their Opening Game," *New-York Tribune*, Thursday, April 23, 1891; "Boston Defeats New-York," *New-York Times*, April 23, 1891, p. 2.

51 Freedman: Hardy, *The New York Giants Base Ball Club*, p. 154; Hynd, *The Giants of the Polo Grounds*, p. 88; Donald Dewey and Nicholas Acocella, *The Biographical History of Baseball* (New York: Carroll & Graf, 1995), p. 152.

51 Baltimore Orioles: James, *The Bill James Historical Abstract*, pp. 38–40; Joseph Durso, *Casey & Mr. McGraw* (St. Louis: The Sporting News, 1989), pp. 31–32.

51–52 Brush: Ivor-Campbell, ed., *Baseball's First Stars*, p. 14 (biographical entry by Rich Eldred).

52–53 Hot dogs: "Hot Dog Born at Polo Grounds," Discovery Channel Online (http://eagle.online.discovery.com/DCO/doc/1012/world/birthday/birthday042996/birthday.html).

53–54 "Take Me Out to the Ballgame": John W. Ripley, "Baseball's Greatest Song," *American Heritage*, June-July 1983, p. 76.

54–55 Forfeits: "Giants Forfeit Game: 'Fans' Disappointed: New York Club Bars Umpire Johnstone from Polo Grounds," *New York Times*, Wednesday, August 8, 1906, p. 4; "Baseball Crowd Causes Forfeit," *New York Times*, Friday, April 12, 1907, p. 10.

55–60 1908 pennant race/Merkle's Boner: John B. Foster, ed., *Spalding's Official Base Ball Guide, 1909* (New York: American Sports Publishing Co., 1909), pp. 97–113; Lawrence S. Ritter, *The Glory of Their Times* (New York: Collier Books, 1966), p. 98; "Baseball Games Played in Garden: Local Fans Witness Reproduction of the Chicago-Pittsburg Doubleheader," *New York Times*, Monday, September 7, 1908, p. 6; "Blunder Costs Giants Victory: Merkle Rushes Off Base Line Before Winning Run Is Scored, and Is Declared Out: Confusion on Ball Field," *New York Times*, Thursday, September 24, 1908, p. 7; description of arrangement of lights: "Fans at the Polo Grounds: Five Thousand Enthusiasts Witness Reproduction of the Game," *New York Times*, Monday, October 5, 1908, p. 8; "Disputed Game Case Remains Undecided," *New York Times*, Tuesday, October 6, 1908, p. 10; "Pulliam's Tie Game Decision Upheld," *New York Times*, Wednesday, October 7, 1908, p. 7; "Giants and Cubs in Final Battle: National League Championship Will Be Decided To-Day at Polo Grounds," *New York Times*, Thursday, October 8, 1908, p. 7; "Giants Bow to Bitter Defeat," *New-York Tribune*, Friday, October 9, 1908, p. 1; "As Seen from Coogan's Bluff: Thousands Watch Corner of Playing Field and Enjoy Baseball Atmosphere," *New-York*

Tribune, October 9, 1908, p. 5; "Forty Thousand See Giants' Hope for Pennant Die," *The World*, October 9, 1908, p. 1; "Jam at the Gates: Spectator Killed," *The World*, October 9, 1908, p. 2; "The Cubs Win the Pennant," *New York Times*, October 9, 1908, p. 2; "Up on Coogan's Bluff: Four Hours with the Unseeing but Anxiously Listening Thousands" by W. J. Lampton, and "How Joy's Mirage Turned to Gloom," *New York Times*, October 9, 1908, p. 2.

60 Expansion of Polo Grounds: John T. Brush, "The Evolution of the Baseball Grandstand: A New Era in the Development of the National Game," *Baseball Magazine*, April 1912, p. 2.

61–62 Fire: Fred Lieb, *Baseball As I Have Known It* (New York: Coward, McCann & Geoghegan, Inc., 1977), p. 35; "Polo Grounds Swept by Fire," *New York Times*, Friday, April 14, 1911, p. 1; Paskert's catch: "Phillies Flay 'Big Six's' Pitching," *NewYork Times*, Friday, April 14, 1911, p. 2.

Chapter 6—A Grand New Stadium

Page

63–66 Rebuilding of Polo Grounds: Lowry, *Green Cathedrals* (SABR), p. 18; Lawrence S. Ritter, *Lost Ballparks* (New York: Viking Studio Books, 1992), p. 161; Hynd, *The Giants of the Polo Grounds*, p. 163; Brush, "The Evolution of the Baseball Grandstand," p. 3; "The Stadium for the New York Baseball Club," *Engineering Record*, July 29, 1911, pp. 126–127; Allan Sangree, "No More War in Baseball: Great Conflicts in the History of the Game, Part II," *Baseball Magazine*, September 1911, pp. 24–25; John Foster, "The Magnificent New Polo Grounds: The Greatest Ball Park in the World," *Baseball Magazine*, October 1911, p. 102; Henry B. Herts, "Grand Stand for the Polo Grounds," *Architecture and Building*, November 1912, p. 457; *Scenes on the Polo Grounds*, a commemorative booklet issued by the New York Giants in 1914; "Giants Will Play on Hilltop To-Day," *New York Times*, Saturday, April 15, 1911, p. 8; "Giants Get Lease on Polo Grounds," *New York Times*, Sunday, April 23, 1911, p. C5; "Polo Grounds Ready," *New York Times*, Sunday, June 25, 1911, p. C5; "Giants Reopen Polo Grounds and Win," *New York Times*, Thursday, June 29, 1911, p. 9.

67 Roof-clearing home runs: "Cleveland Takes Yanks into Camp,"*New York Times*, Thursday, June 5, 1913, p. 9; "Ruth Wallops Out His 28th Home Run: Terrific Crash Over the Polo Grounds Stands Sets New World's Record," *New York Times*, Thursday, September 25, 1919, p. 10.

68–69 Snodgrass quote on Charlie Faust: Ritter, *The Glory of Their Times*, pp. 95–97; "Tailenders Down Champions, 5 to 2: Donlin's Home Run and Drucke's Wildness Decide Game—Faust Pitches One Inning," *New York Times*, Sunday, October 8, 1911, p. C5; "Giants Close Their Season with Defeat," *New York Times*, Friday, October 13, 1911, p. 12.

69–70 Winning streaks: "Giants' Sixteenth Straight Victory: And Marquard Records His Nineteenth, Remaining Undefeated This Year," *New York Times*, Thursday, July 4, 1912, p. 8; "Marquard Driven from Box by Cubs," *New York Times*, Tuesday, July 9, 1912, p. 10; "Giants Continue Victorious March, Taking Seventeenth Straight Game," *New York Times*, Tuesday, May 30, 1916, p. 10; "Giants Set Record for Straight Victories with Twenty-One," *New York Times*, Tuesday, September 26, 1916, p. 12; "Braves End Flare of Giants' Meteor," *New York Times*, Sunday, October 1, 1916, p. S1.

71–73 Sunday baseball in New York: Harold Seymour, *Baseball: The Golden Age* (New York: Oxford University Press, 1971), p. 364; "Giants and Yankees to Clash for Titanic Fund: Game Will Be Played at the Polo Grounds at Three o'Clock To-Morrow," *New-York Tribune*, Saturday, April 20, 1912, p. 10; "Baseball for the Titanic Fund," *New-York Tribune*,

Sunday, April 21, 1912, p. 10; "14,083 Fans See Game for Charity: Giants Defeat Yankees at Polo Grounds for Benefit of Titanic Survivors," *New York Times*, Monday, April 22, 1912, p. 12; "Benefit for 69th Today: Soldiers to See Baseball Game and Hear Polo Grounds Concert," *New York Times*, Sunday, August 19, 1917, p. S3; "Giants Break Before Attack of the Reds" by "Igoe," *The World*, Monday, August 20, 1917, p. 8; "Reds Apply Whitewash Brush to the Giants in Benefit Game," *New York Times*, August 20, 1917, p. 10; "Hale McGraw and Matty to Court," *The World*, Tuesday, August 21, 1917, p. 6; "Managers Must Explain Sunday Game to Court: McGraw and Matty Summoned for Playing Ball at 69th Benefit" by W. J. Macbeth, *New York Tribune*, August 21, 1917, p. 13; "Sunday Baseball Charge Dismissed: Magistrate McQuade, in Discharging Matty and McGraw, Says They Deserved Praise, Not a Summons," *The World*, Wednesday, August 22, 1917, p. 8; "McQuade Dismisses Case of McGraw and Matty," *New York Tribune*, August 22, 1917, p. 13; "Signs Sunday Movie Bill: Sunday Baseball Measure Also Approved by Gov. Smith," *New York Times*, Sunday, April 20, 1919, p. 10; "Advent of Sunday Baseball Draws 60,000 Persons to Polo Grounds and Ebbets Field: Fill Polo Grounds for Sunday Battle," *New York Times*, Monday, May 5, 1919, p. 14.

73–74 Quick games: "Giants and Phillies Play Record Game," *New York Times*, Tuesday, October 7, 1913, p. 11; "Giants Waste No Time on Dodgers," *New York Times*, Saturday, August 31, 1918, p. 5; "Giants Finish with Pair of Victories," *New York Times*, Monday, September 29, 1919, p. 9.

74 Wood: "Old Giant Rooter Hushed by Death" by Broun, p. 10.

74–75 New ownership: Hynd, *The Giants of the Polo Grounds*, p. 210; Fred Stein and Nick Peters, *Giants Diary* (Berkeley, CA: North Atlantic Books), pp. 38–39; Charles C. Alexander, *John McGraw* (New York: Viking Penguin, Inc., 1988), p. 210; "Chas. A. Stoneham, Giants' Owner, Dies," *New York Times*, Tuesday, January 7, 1936, p. 21.

75 Chapman: "Chapman Suffers Skull Fracture: Cleveland Shortstop Victim of Severe Injury When Hit by Pitched Ball," *New York Times*, Tuesday, August 17, 1920, p. 14; "Ray Chapman Dies: Mays Exonerated," *New York Times*, Wednesday, August 18, 1920, p. 15; "Chapman Dies: Mays Absolved of All Blame" by W. O. McGeehan, *New York Tribune*, August 18, 1920, p. 1 (source of Mays quote).

75 Powers: Mike Shatzkin, ed., *The Ballplayers* (New York: Arbor House, 1990); Dewey and Acocella, *The Biographical History of Baseball*, p. 365; Rich Westcott, *Philadelphia's Old Ballparks* (Philadelphia: Temple University Press, 1996), pp. 110–111; "Chance for Catcher Powers to Recover," *Philadelphia Public Ledger*, Thursday, April 15, 1909, p. 6; "Dr. Powers Loses Fight with Death: Athletics' Plucky Catcher Was Injured in First Game at Shibe Park," *Philadelphia Public Ledger*, Tuesday, April 27, 1909, p. 2. (The version that Powers died of injuries from crashing into a wall in the season opener is cited in *The Ballplayers* and *The Biographical History of Baseball.* The version that he dislocated his intestine in the season opener is cited in the April 27 *Public Ledger*. The version that the problems started with indigestion from eating a cheese sandwich before the season opener is cited in *Philadelphia's Old Ballparks* and in the April 15 *Public Ledger.)*

Chapter 7—Home Runs and Hubbell

Page

90 Attendance: *The Dope Book*, compiled by J. G. Taylor Spink in collaboration with Paul A. Rickart and Clifford Kachline (St. Louis: The Sporting News, 1959); "Throng of 38,600 at Polo Grounds: Crowd Shatters Attendance Record Made in 1911, and 10,000 Are Turned Away: Indians Thrash Yankees," *New York Times*, Monday, May 17, 1920, p. 11.

90–91 Yankees leaving the Polo Grounds: Seymour, *Baseball: The Golden Age*, p. 55; "Yanks Lose Home at Polo Grounds: Owners of Giants Decline to Allow Further Joint Occupancy After This Year," *New York Times*, Saturday, May 15, 1920, p. 18; "Discuss Ousting of Yanks: Herrmann and Johnson Confer with Stoneham and McGraw," *New York Times*, Friday, May 21, 1920, p. 11; "Hunt for Home Is Spared to Yanks: Eviction Order Rescinded After Chat Between Giants' Officials and Ban Johnson," *New York Times*, Saturday, May 22, 1920, p. 19; "Baseball's Biggest Park Will Be Dedicated To-Day by the Fans" by "Monitor," *The World*, Wednesday, April 18, 1923; "Babe Did It; 74,000 Saw Him and Yanks Beat Red Sox, 4–1" by Heywood Broun, *The World*, Thursday, April 19, 1923.

91–92 Extension of grandstands/stadium expansion: Ritter, *Lost Ballparks*, pp. 163–165; Lowry, *Green Cathedrals* (SABR), p. 66; "Capacity of 50,000 for Polo Grounds," *New York Herald*, Friday, October 21, 1921; "New Concrete Bleachers for the Polo Grounds," *New York Herald*, Wednesday, July 26, 1922; "New Grandstand Planned for the Polo Grounds," *New York Herald*, Tuesday, August 22, 1922; "Polo Grounds Clubhouse Gives Way to Progress" by W. O. McGeehan, *New York Herald*, Tuesday, November 21, 1922; "Champion Giants Come into Their Own Here To-Day: McGraw and His Team Will Welcome 41,000 Fans at Opening of 'New' Polo Grounds" by "Monitor," *The World*, Thursday, April 26, 1923, p. 8; "Polo Grounds Damage Suit," *New York Times*, Friday, December 28, 1923; interview with Phil Lowry, December 18, 1997.

92–93 Grant monument: Lawrence S. Ritter, *East Side-West Side: Tales of New York Sporting Life, 1910-1960* (New York: Total Sports, 1998), pp. 10–11; Lowry, *Green Cathedrals* (SABR), p. 66; "Capt. Eddie Grant Memorial Unveiled," *New York Herald*, Tuesday, May 31, 1921.

93–94 Overhang: Lowry, *Green Cathedrals* (Addison-Wesley), pp. 198–199; Stein, *Under Coogan's Bluff*, p. 2; correspondence with John Pastier, 1997–98.

94 Harlem River Speedway: Moscow, *The Street Book*, p. 57; "Brushing on Speedway," *New York Times*, Monday, April 22, 1912, p. 12.

95 Watching from Coogan's Bluff: Durso, *The Days of Mr. McGraw*, pp. 223–224.

96–97 Terry: Dewey and Acocella, *The Biographical History of Baseball*, p. 463.

97–98 Ott: Fred Stein, "No Cheap Homers for Ott," *Baseball Research Journal*, 20 (1991), pp. 70–72.

98 Bankhead: Stein, *Under Coogan's Bluff*, pp. 8–9.

99–100 Night baseball: "Giants to Install Lighting System," *New York Sun*, Thursday, October 26, 1939; "Giants' Lights Most Costly," *New York Sun*, Monday, November 6, 1939; "Giants Dispel Polo Grounds Gloom," *New York Sun*, Wednesday, November 15, 1939; "Giants Will Play Night Baseball Here: Lighting Plans Set for Polo Grounds" by John Drebinger, *New York Times*, November 15, 1939, p. 31; "Night Ball at Polo Grounds," *New York Daily Mirror*, November 15, 1939; "Giants Turn On Lights Tonight for Nocturnal Bow Against Bees" by Arthur J. Daley, *New York Times*, Friday, May 24, 1940; "22,260 See Giants Rout Bees in Night Baseball Inaugural at Polo Grounds" by John Drebinger, *New York Times*, Saturday, May 25, 1940, p. 12.

100 1942 All Star Game: David Pietrusza, "Controversy Mars First Night All-Star Game," *USA Today Baseball Weekly*, July 7, 1993, p. 41; "American League All-Stars Win on Homers by Boudreau and York in First" by John Drebinger, *New York Times*, Tuesday, July 7, 1942, p. 23; "City Blacked Out for Second Time, Though Not 100%: Polo Grounds Game Lasts Till 9:28, So Crowd Stays, Sings Till Lights Go On," *New York Times*, July 7, 1942, p. 1.

100 Three-sided game: W. G. Nicholson, "Three-Dimensional Baseball" (source and date

unknown); "50,000 Fans See Dodgers Triumph: Flock Tallies Five Runs to One for Yankees, None for Giants in Bond Game" by John Drebinger, *New York Times*, Tuesday, June 27, 1944, p. 22.

101 Changes in the Polo Grounds: Ritter, *Lost Ballparks*, p. 165; Stein, *Under Coogan's Bluff*, p. 2; John Lardner, "The Purging of the Walls," *Newsweek*, February 23, 1948, p. 76; "3 Old IRT Yards Are Put on Block," *New York Sun*, Saturday, December 11, 1948.

101–102 Plaques: Seymour, *Baseball: The Golden Age*, p. 364; Bob Carroll, Michael Gershman, David Neft, and John Thorn, eds., *Total Football* (New York: HarperCollins Publishers, 1997), pp. 221–222; "After the Unveiling of the Plaque," *New York Sun*, Monday, December 3, 1945; "Walker Plaque Unveiled," *New York Times*, Monday, July 12, 1948, p. 13; "Walker Plaque at the Polo Grounds," *New York Sun*, Wednesday, June 16, 1948.

102 Exit policy change: "Chandler Orders Indefinite Ban After Row with Polo Grounds Fan," *New York Sun*, Friday, April 29, 1949; "Fans at Polo Grounds Obey New Rule to Keep Off Field" by Frank C. True, *New York Sun*, Wednesday, May 4, 1949; correspondence with Stan Isaacs, March 1998.

102–103 Maintaining the field: "Polo Grounds Has Face Lift," *New York Sun*, Thursday, October 18, 1945.

103–104 Schwab: "Dig, Dig, Dig," *The New Yorker*, April 12, 1947, p. 24; Tom Meany, "Family Here Lives in the Polo Grounds," *Collier's*, July 6, 1956, p. 46; Noel Hynd, "Found: Charming 2BR, 1Bth Apt. in the Leftfield Stands," *Sports Illustrated*, October 20, 1986, p. 6; "Adieus Prove Difficult for Men Behind the Scenes at Polo Grounds" by Joseph M. Sheehan, *New York Times*, Monday, September 30, 1957, p. 36; interview with Jerry Schwab, December 14, 1997.

104–105 Negro Leagues: Donn Rogosin, *Invisible Men: Life in Baseball's Negro Leagues* (New York: Atheneum, 1983), pp. 110–113; Robert Peterson, *Only the Ball Was White* (New York: Prentice-Hall, Inc., 1970); James A. Riley, *The Biographical Encyclopedia of the Negro Baseball Leagues* (New York: Carroll & Graf Publishers, Inc., 1994); Dick Clark and Larry Lester, eds., *The Negro Leagues Book* (Cleveland: Society for American Baseball Research, 1994); "Kansas City on Top, 2–1: Downs Newark Eagles in First Game of Negro World Series," *New York Times*, Wednesday, September 18, 1946, p. 34; "Negro Series to Start: Cubans Meet Cleveland Team at Polo Grounds Tonight," *New York Times*, Friday, September 19, 1947, p. 32; "Negro Champions Tie: Cubans, Buckeyes, 5–5, When Rain Halts Opener of Series," *New York Times*, Saturday, September 20, 1947, p. 19.

105 Integration of Giants: Peterson, *Only the Ball Was White*, p. 201; "Giants Get Two Negro Players in Move to Strengthen Line-up," *New York Times*, Wednesday, July 6, 1949, p. 32; "Dodgers Down Giants Before 34,468" by Joseph M. Sheehan, *New York Times*, Saturday, July 9, 1949, p. 16.

Chapter 8—The Final Years

Page

107 Mays: Willie Mays with Lou Sahadi, *Say Hey: The Autobiography of Willie Mays* (New York: Simon and Schuster, 1988), p. 42; "Spahn Turns Back Durocher Men, 4–1," *New York Times*, Tuesday, May 29, 1951, p. 29.

108–109 Pennant race and Thomson home run: "Giants Capture Pennant, Beating Dodgers 5–4 in 9th on Thomson's 3-Run Homer" by John Drebinger, *New York Times*, Thursday, October 4, 1951, p. 1; John McCormack editorial letter in *Dallas Morning News*, Sunday, August 16, 1987; correspondence with John Pastier, 1997–98.

109–111 1954 World Series: "Giants Win in 10th from Indians, 5–2, on Rhodes' Homer" by John Drebinger, *New York Times*, Thursday, October 4, 1951, p. 1; Lowry, *Green Cathedrals* (SABR), p. 65; correspondence with John Pastier, 1997–98; Arnold Hano, *A Day in the Bleachers* (New York: Da Capo Press, 1955); "One Sunny Day: Memory Is Still Green" by Josh Getlin, *Los Angeles Times*, Tuesday, October 9, 1984, p. II-1; conversation with Ted Hathaway, January 1998.

111 New York fans: Stein, *Under Coogan's Bluff*, pp. 7–8.

111–112 Jones and Stubing: Author's conversation with Deacon Jones and Moose Stubing, August 2, 1998.

112–113 National League abandonment of New York: Jack Orr, "The Polo Grounds," *Sport*, September 1953, p. 54; "Mystery Bullet Kills Baseball Fan in Midst of Crowd at Polo Grounds," *New York Times*, Wednesday, July 5, 1950, p. 1; Hogrogian, "The Polo Grounds Case: Part II," p. 5; Paul Ferrante, "The Polo Grounds: Once Maligned, Now Most-Wanted by Stadia Collectors," *Sports Collectors Digest*, February 20, 1998, p. 132; Stein and Peters, *Giants Diary*, p. 121; "New Look in Minneapolis," *Sports Illustrated*, August 20, 1956, p. 36.

114 Final New York Giants game: Durso, *The Days of Mr. McGraw*, p. 225; "The New York Giants: 1883–1957" by Milton Bracker, *New York Times*, Monday, September 30, 1957, p. 1; "Giants, in Farewell to New York, Lose to Pirates Before Crowd of 11,606," *New York Times*, September 30, 1957, p. 36.

115–118 Birth of the Mets/demise of the Polo Grounds: Leonard Schecter, *Once upon the Polo Grounds* (New York: The Dial Press, 1970); "Polo Grounds Doomed to Make Way for Low-Rent Housing Project" by Charles G. Bennett, *New York Times*, Friday, March 10, 1961, p. 1; "Polo Grounds to Go, but Not the Memories," *New York Times*, March 10, 1961, p. 56; "City Stadium Bill Upset at Albany in Queens Revolt" by Layhmond Robinson, *New York Times*, Thursday, March 16, 1961, p. 1; "Assembly Passes Bill for Stadium Under Pressure" by Layhmond Robinson, *New York Times*, Friday, March 17, 1961, p. 1; "Yanks Reluctant to Rent Stadium to New Team: Polo Grounds Use Is Recommended" by John Drebinger, *New York Times*, Monday, March 20, 1961, p. 38; "Good-by to a Ball Park," *Newsweek*, March 20, 1961, p. 28; Robert Shaplen, "How to Build a Ball Club," *Sports Illustrated*, March 5, 1962, p. 39; "National League Baseball Returns to City Today When Mets Play Pirates: Pomp Is Planned at Polo Grounds" by Robert L. Teague, *New York Times*, Friday, April 13, 1962, p. 41; "Mets Flounder in Mud at Polo Grounds and Drop Home Debut to Pirates, 4–3" by Louis Effrat, *New York Times*, Saturday, April 14, 1962, p. 18; "Remodelled," *The New Yorker*, April 14, 1962, p. 34; "Payment Sought for Polo Grounds" by John Sibley, *New York Times*, Wednesday, September 18, 1963, p. 41.

117 Throneberry: "Homer and Misplays Top Mets, 8–7, 4–3, at Polo Grounds" by Robert M. Lipsyte, *New York Times*, Monday, June 18, 1962, p. 30.

117–118 Brock and Aaron home runs: "Brock of Cubs Hits Bleachers 460 Feet Away," *New York Times*, Monday, June 18, 1962, p. 30; "Braves Hand Mets 7th Loss in Row: Jay Hook Routed in 7-to-1 Defeat: Hank Aaron of Braves Hits a 460-Foot Grand-Slam Homer Off Met Hurler" by Robert M. Lipsyte, *New York Times*, Tuesday, June 19, 1962, p. 38.

118 Final games: "Mets Beat Cubs, 2–1, in Farewell to Baseball at the Polo Grounds" by Robert M. Lipsyte, *New York Times*, Monday, September 24, 1962, p. 39; "With Proper Finality" by Arthur Daley, *New York Times*, Wednesday, September 18, 1963, p. 44; "Era of Mets Ends at Polo Grounds" by Gordon S. White, Jr., *New York Times*, Thursday, September 19, 1963, p. 32.

119 Demolition: "'Neath Coogan's Bluff Hammer Falls Where Giants Stood 10 Feet Tall" by Martin Arnold, *New York Times*, Saturday, April 11, 1964, p. 27.

119 Parting comments: George Tinker, "A Nostalgic Look at the Polo Grounds," *The Ballparks Bulletin,* May 1986; Roger Angell, "The Sporting Scene," *The New Yorker,* May 25, 1963, p. 142.

Chapter 9—Boxing to Buffalo Bill

Page

135 Final football game: "Bills Down Jets in Finale, 19–10, and Tie for Lead" by Deane McGowen, *New York Times,* Sunday, December 15, 1963, p. 1.

135 Wismer ploy: Philip J. Lowry, *Green Gridirons* (North Huntingdon, Pa.; Professional Football Researchers Association, 1990), p. 43.

136–137 Grange: "Red Grange Leads Bears to Victory in Pro Debut Here as 70,000 Look On" by Richard Vidmer, *New York Times,* Monday, December 7, 1925, p. 26.

137 Sneakers game: "55,000 Expected to Watch Bears in Game Against Giants at Polo Grounds" by Robert F. Kelley, *New York Times,* Sunday, December 9, 1934, p. S3; "National Pro Football Title Is Won by Giants in Game Jammed with Thrills" by Robert F. Kelley, and "Basketball Shoes Prove Big Aid to the Giants on Frozen Gridiron" by Walter Fleisher, *New York Times,* Monday, December 10, 1934, p. 25.

138–139 APFA games: "All-Americans Win Pro Gridiron Game: Buffalo Eleven Victor in Close Match with Thorpe's Bulldogs—Score, 7–3," *New York Times,* Sunday, December 5, 1920, p. S1; "Thorpe's Pro Team Beats Giants, 17–0: Tigers Crush Brickley's Eleven in One-Sided Game—Small Crowd at Polo Grounds," *New York Times,* Sunday, December 4, 1921, p. S2.

139 College football: "Army-Navy Game at the Polo Grounds To-Day," *New York Times,* Saturday, November 29, 1913, p. 10; "Navy Football Team Favorite Over Army in To-Day's Gridiron Battle," *The World,* November 29, 1913, p. 8; "Army Smothers Annapolis Team by 22–9 Score," *New York Times,* Sunday, November 30, 1913;"Polo Grounds as Football Center," *New York Sun,* Thursday, October 26, 1939.

139–140 Notre Dame: Murray Sperber, *Shake Down the Thunder: The Creation of Notre Dame Football* (New York: Henry Holt and Company, 1993), pp. 47–48, 181; "Notre Dame's Cyclone Beats Army, 13 to 7," by Grantland Rice, *New York Herald Tribune,* Sunday, October 19, 1924, p. 1.

140–141 Boxing: Gerald Suster, *Champions of the Ring: The Lives and Times of Boxing's Heavyweight Heroes* (London: Robson Books, 1992); Jersey Jones, "Remembering the Polo Grounds: Historic 75-Year-Old Baseball Park, in Which Much Boxing History Was Made, Finally Passes from the Sports Scene," *The Ring,* July 1964, pp. 26–27; "Louis, Near Defeat, Stops Conn in 13th and Retains Crown" by James P. Dawson, *New York Times,* Thursday, June 19, 1941, p. 1.

141 Buffalo Bill: "Buffalo Bill Gives a Party: Entertaining His Friends with Roast Buffalo at the Polo Grounds," *New-York Times,* Monday, June 16, 1884, p. 5; "Buffalo Bill at the Polo Grounds," *New-York Times,* Tuesday, June 17, 1884, p. 2.

142–143 Other events: "Polo Grounds Will Have Opera Season," *New York Herald,* Monday, April 2, 1923; "Opera Stage to Be Frigate and Polo Grounds a Harbor," *New York Herald Tribune,* Friday, June 12, 1925, p. 10; "Old New York in Pictures—No. 587—Tobogganing at the Polo Grounds," *New York Sun,* Friday, August 15, 1930; "Leaping Skiers Replace Giants" by Will Wedge, *New York Sun,* Saturday, February 13, 1937; "Ski Jumping and Racing Will Feature Three-Day Carnival at Polo Grounds: Winter Carnival Starts Saturday," *New York Times*, Sunday, February 14, 1937, p. 6; "Third Rail Kills Bull," *New York Sun*, Monday, July 13, 1942; "10 Hurt at Rodeo as Car Skids," *New York Sun*, Wednesday, July 15, 1942; "Army Blasts Village in Show at Polo Grounds," *New York Herald Tribune*, Sunday, September 20, 1942, p. 19; "75,000 at Polo Grounds Hear Archbishop in Prayer for Rome," *New York Herald Tribune*, Monday, October 4, 1943, p. 1; "Auto Racing for Polo Grounds" by Herbert Goren, *New York Sun*, Wednesday, November 26, 1947; "Midgets Invade Ball Park," *Popular Science*, August 1948, p. 94.

Appendix A—Polo Grounds Park Factors

Page

145 Park effects: John Holway, *The Sluggers* (Alexandria, Va.: A Redefinition Book, 1989), p. 64; Thorn and Palmer, eds., *Total Baseball*, Fourth Edition, pp. 2236–2237; author's correspondence with John McCormack, December 1997.

146–148 Home-road breakdowns and run and home run factors: Thorn and Palmer, eds., *Total Baseball* (1989), pp. 2207–2211; author's correspondence with John Pastier.

148–149 Overhang: Author's correspondence with John McCormack, December 1997.

Appendix B—Summary of Championship Events and Other Highlights at the Polo Grounds

Page

151–152 Boxing: International Boxing Research Organization.

152–154 NFL title games: Carroll, Gershman, Neft, and Thorn, eds., *Total Football*, pp. 122–126.

154–161 World Series: Lansche, *The Forgotten Championships*, pp. 6–52, and *Glory Fades Away*, pp. 38–159; Craig Carter, ed., *Official World Series Records* (St. Louis: The Sporting News, 1979); "Giants Win, 2–1: Devore Snatches Victory in Ninth," *New York Times*, Friday, October 11, 1912, p. 1; "Yanks Win, 18–4; Tie Series: Roosevelt Delays Date to Stick to End," *New York Post*, Friday, October 2, 1936, p. 2; "Yanks Crush Giants, 18–4, a World Series Record; 45,000 See Second Game: Fans Cheer Roosevelt and Remain Till He Leaves at End" by John Drebinger, *New York Times*, Saturday, October 3, 1936, pp. 1, 10.

161–163 Multiteam doubleheaders: "Clev'land and Grays Play Here Saturday," *Pittsburgh Courier*, Saturday, May 7, 1932, p. 1; Game-by-game research of 1883 to 1885 seasons from the *New-York Times*; "New York and Brooklyn Quit Even on the Day—Rowdyism in Morning Game," *New York Times*, Tuesday, September 8, 1903, p.10.

163–164 Plaques: Author's correspondence with Everett Parker, July 1998; "A Piece of Polo Grounds History Cast in Iron" by Stuart Leeds, *Giants Jottings* (publication of the New York Giants Historical Society), vol. 1, no. 3 (July 1999), p. 6.

Index

Italicized page entries indicate photos.